If, By Miracle

THE AZRIELI SERIES OF HOLOCAUST SURVIVOR MEMOIRS: PREVIOUSLY PUBLISHED TITLES

ENGLISH TITLES

Album of My Life by Ann Szedlecki
Bits and Pieces by Henia Reinhartz
A Drastic Turn of Destiny by Fred Mann
E/96: Fate Undecided by Paul-Henri Rips
Fleeing from the Hunter by Marian Domanski
From Generation to Generation by Agnes Tomasov
Gatehouse to Hell by Felix Opatowski
Getting Out Alive by Tommy Dick
If Home Is Not Here by Max Bornstein
Knocking on Every Door by Anka Voticky
Little Girl Lost by Betty Rich
Memories from the Abyss by William Tannenzapf/ *But I Had a Happy Childhood* by
   Renate Krakauer
The Shadows Behind Me by Willie Sterner
Spring's End by John Freund
Survival Kit by Zuzana Sermer
Tenuous Threads by Judy Abrams/ *One of the Lucky Ones*
   by Eva Felsenburg Marx
Under the Yellow and Red Stars by Alex Levin
The Violin by Rachel Shtibel/ *A Child's Testimony* by Adam Shtibel

TITRES FRANÇAIS

L'Album de ma vie par Ann Szedlecki
Cachée par Marguerite Elias Quddus
Étoile jaune, étoile rouge par Alex Levin
La Fin du printemps par John Freund
Fragments de ma vie par Henia Reinhartz
Frapper à toutes les portes par Anka Voticky
De génération en génération par Agnes Tomasov
Matricule E/96 par Paul-Henri Rips
Objectif : survivre par Tommy Dick
Souvenirs de l'abîme par William Tannenzapf/ *Le Bonheur de l'innocence* par
   Renate Krakauer
Un terrible revers de fortune par Fred Mann
Traqué par Marian Domanski
Le Violon par Rachel Shtibel/ *Témoignage d'un enfant* par Adam Shtibel

If, By Miracle
Michael Kutz

TRANSLATED FROM YIDDISH BY VIVIAN FELSEN

Maxine

From Michael Kutz

THE AZRIELI FOUNDATION
www.azrielifoundation.org

Cover and book design by Mark Goldstein
Endpaper maps by Martin Gilbert
Maps on pages xxviii-xxix by François Blanc
Photo on page 132 courtesy of Yad Vashem
Translated from Yiddish by Vivian Felsen

LIBRARY AND ARCHIVES CANADA CATALOGUING IN PUBLICATION

Kutz, Michael, 1930–
    If, by miracle/ Michael Kutz.

(Azrieli series of Holocaust survivor memoirs. Series v)
Includes bibliographical references and index.
ISBN 978-1-897470-35-0

1. Kutz, Michael, 1930–. 2. Holocaust, Jewish (1939–1945) – Poland – Personal narratives. 3. Jewish children in the Holocaust – Poland – Biography. 4. Holocaust survivors – Canada – Biography. I. Title. II. Series: Azrieli series of Holocaust survivor memoirs. Series v

DS135.P63K88 2013   940.53'18092   C2013-901380-6

MIX
From responsible
sources
FSC   FSC® C004191
www.fsc.org

PRINTED IN CANADA

The Azrieli Series of Holocaust Survivor Memoirs

Contents

Series Preface:
In their own words...

In telling these stories, the writers have liberated themselves. For so many years we did not speak about it, even when we became free people living in a free society. Now, when at last we are writing about what happened to us in this dark period of history, knowing that our stories will be read and live on, it is possible for us to feel truly free. These unique historical documents put a face on what was lost, and allow readers to grasp the enormity of what happened to six million Jews – one story at a time.

David J. Azrieli, C.M., C.Q., M.Arch
Holocaust survivor and founder, The Azrieli Foundation

Since the end of World War II, over 30,000 Jewish Holocaust survivors have immigrated to Canada. Who they are, where they came from, what they experienced and how they built new lives for themselves and their families are important parts of our Canadian heritage. The Azrieli Foundation's Holocaust Survivor Memoirs Program was established to preserve and share the memoirs written by those who survived the twentieth-century Nazi genocide of the Jews of Europe and later made their way to Canada. The program is guided by the conviction that each survivor of the Holocaust has a remarkable story to tell, and that such stories play an important role in education about tolerance and diversity.

Millions of individual stories are lost to us forever. By preserving the stories written by survivors and making them widely available to a broad audience, the Azrieli Foundation's Holocaust Survivor Memoirs Program seeks to sustain the memory of all those who perished at the hands of hatred, abetted by indifference and apathy. The personal accounts of those who survived against all odds are as different as the people who wrote them, but all demonstrate the courage, strength, wit and luck that it took to prevail and survive in such terrible adversity. The memoirs are also moving tributes to people – strangers and friends – who risked their lives to help others, and who, through acts of kindness and decency in the darkest of moments, frequently helped the persecuted maintain faith in humanity and courage to endure. These accounts offer inspiration to all, as does the survivors' desire to share their experiences so that new generations can learn from them.

The Holocaust Survivor Memoirs Program collects, archives and publishes these distinctive records and the print editions are available free of charge to libraries, educational institutions and Holocaust-education programs across Canada, and at Azrieli Foundation educational events. They are also available for sale to the general public at bookstores.

The Azrieli Foundation would like to express appreciation to the following people for their invaluable efforts in producing this book: Sherry Dodson (Maracle Press), Sir Martin Gilbert, Farla Klaiman, Naama Shilo from the photo archive department at Yad Vashem, Mia Spiro, and Margie Wolfe and Emma Rodgers of Second Story Press.

About the Glossary

The following memoir contains a number of terms, concepts and historical references that may be unfamiliar to the reader. For information on major organizations; significant historical events and people; geographical locations; religious and cultural terms; and foreign-language words and expressions that will help give context and background to the events described in the text, please see the glossary beginning on page 99.

Introduction

Except for the graves of my family and my few survivor friends, I no longer felt any attachment to Nieśwież.

In the summer of 1945, when Michael Kutz realized that his whole family had been wiped out, that there was no one left, he began a long journey in search of a new home. That summer marked the end of his youth in Nieśwież, a small town in present-day Belarus, ninety-five kilometres south of the capital, Minsk. The orphaned fourteen-year-old recognized that alongside his family, a whole world was gone – the world now often compressed into the word *shtetl*: a town populated by a tightly knit Jewish community, its geography shaped by synagogues and religious schools, and its daily chatter inflected by competing visions of where and how Jews should live – in the ancient homeland or within other societies around the world. The Nazi genocide had eradicated one of the possibilities; there were no more Jews in Nieśwież at the end of World War II.

Michael Kutz wrote his memoirs late in life and the sweeping breadth of his story takes us on a journey through twentieth-century Eastern European, Soviet, global, Canadian and Jewish history. Born in 1930 into a family of five, young Michael grew up in a decade that thoroughly transformed Jewish life in eastern Poland. Jews in the region struggled to maintain individual lives and communal cohesion amidst Europe-wide arguments about the status of national minorities, strong currents of antisemitism in Poland, increased overall secularization and urbanization, and, by the end of the decade, annexation and war.

Michael Kutz's description of life in his hometown of Nieśwież gives the reader a window onto these times. With a population of almost 7,000 inhabitants, among them some 4,000 Jews, Nieśwież exemplified the crystallized image of a shtetl and its transformation in the interwar period: a small Eastern European town with a strong Jewish presence, where Jewish tradesmen and artisans were the driving economic force. The Belorussians and Ukrainians living in the town spoke and understood Yiddish, and much of the daily and weekly life followed the rhythm of Jewish religious observance. Several synagogues and cheders (religious elementary schools) catered to the large Jewish community. The very existence of this community in eastern Poland was the result of restrictions imposed upon the Jewish subjects of the Russian Empire: after 1792, Jews were required to live within the confines of the Pale of Settlement, a region covering large parts of present-day Ukraine, Belorussia, Lithuania, Latvia, eastern Poland and the western parts of Russia. With the 1917 Russian Revolution, these restrictions were lifted and many Jews moved away from the former Pale, but many stayed and became citizens of Poland, the Soviet Union, or the other states that emerged from World War I and thus continued the strong presence of Jews in the area.

Nieśwież fell to Poland in 1918 and, as Michael Kutz describes, its Jewish community experienced the political trends in Polish society characteristic of the time in its very own way. Since the turn of the century, right-wing forces had been on the rise in Poland. This trend intensified during World War I and, again, during the economic crisis of the 1920s and 1930s. At that time, the right-wing nationalist party National Democracy (ND, "Endecja") became an influential political force, and Polish nationalism with an insistence on creating a "Poland of Poles" – i.e., of Catholics – gained traction among major parts of society. The "Endeks" singled out Jews as un-Polish and blamed them for the rising unemployment, frequently calling for boycotts of Jewish businesses and condoning the regular violent attacks on individual Jews. By the mid-1930s, this type of nationalism found expression in state policies that imposed special taxes on Jews and Jewish businesses, prohibited the ritual slaughter required to maintain the Jewish dietary laws (largely to break the monopoly of Jewish butchers on the meat market), introduced entry limitations for Jews to Polish universities, and banished Jewish students to the so-called ghetto benches in the back of classrooms. More and more professional associations were closed to Jews, making it impossible for Jews to conduct business.

Responses and reactions to these restrictions among the Jews were varied and continued a pattern that had developed in the Pale of Settlement and Poland since the late nineteenth century. The increasing industrialization of the economy in the region left many people unemployed or working under dismal conditions. As in other countries, younger people especially rebelled against worker exploitation, authoritarian state rule and patriarchal authority in the family. They joined political movements that sought to curtail capitalist exploitation and establish individual liberties and gender equality, and also championed rights to free religious and cultural self-expression.

Some Jews saw no prospects for a secure Jewish existence in Eastern Europe and turned to Zionism, advocating emigration to the ancient homeland of Israel – then Palestine under Ottoman and, later, British rule. Others joined moderate or radical left parties and youth movements that worked toward an overall revolution and, in part, promoted Jewish participation in pluralist societies. The split between Zionist activists organized in groups such as Betar or Hashomer Hatzair and others who joined the General Jewish Labor Bund in Lithuania, Poland and Russia often divided families and, more often than not, the young from the old. Kutz's parents personify this split, arguing about whether young Michael should be educated in a Yiddish or Hebrew school. The focus on the language of instruction reflects the different political agendas: adherence to the Jewish religion and the vision of the establishment of a Jewish state by learning Hebrew countered the efforts toward integration and secularization articulated in promoting Yiddish.

Within the larger Polish political landscape, the Jewish political parties were looked upon with suspicion and driven underground; many activists were arrested and imprisoned. Promoting emigration was considered a sign of disloyalty, while left-wing activists were suspected of supporting the Soviet Union – tantamount to treason. Belorussians and Ukrainians were also suspected of promoting their own nations' interest and subjected to surveillance and, in many cases, arrest. As a town in the peripheral regions of Poland, the residents of Nieśwież experienced these developments in a somewhat less intense way than those in larger cities and in the centre of Poland, yet Kutz includes enough information to make it clear that their impact on the locals was palpable.

The countries bordering Poland in the east and in the west – the Soviet Union and Germany – also underwent stark political and social transformations in the interwar period. Radical changes in these countries would soon determine Jewish life in Nieśwież and eastern Poland: one in the form of dismantling the institutions and frameworks of collective Jewish existence, the other by posing a lethal threat to individual Jews.

Since its creation in 1922, the USSR had been undergoing major transformations through the industrialization and secularization projects set in motion in the 1920s that reconfigured the social and moral fibre of Soviet society. Many previously marginalized social groups – peasants, workers and national minorities – had welcomed the lifting of restrictions and discriminations that had limited their access to education, disenfranchised them in perpetuity, or, as in the case of Jews, confined them to the Pale of Settlement. The attempts of the Bolshevik government to establish a society of equals that would meet the basic needs of everyone came at a price, however. The plan to re-engineer the social order radicalized over time to such an extent that new hierarchies and forms of violence developed that were detrimental to creating a society allowing for the pursuit of individual rights and liberties while achieving the common good.

Soviet Jews experienced these promising, yet eventually problematic developments in their own way. A brief renaissance of national cultures, such as the one that promoted Jewish culture through state support for publishing, theatre and schooling in Yiddish in the 1920s, soon gave way to an overall reorientation of social and cultural policies toward creating a unified Soviet culture. The secularization campaigns of the 1920s and 1930s, primarily aiming to rid Soviet society of the impact of patriarchal and authoritarian rule rooted in Russian Orthodoxy, targeted Christian, Jewish, Buddhist, and Muslim institutions of worship and communal welfare. For Jews, the closing of synagogues, religious schools and community institutions such as the *kehilla*, the traditional locus of collective self-governance, eradicated the core of their way of life that had followed the religious calendar structured by the Sabbath and important holidays. By the end of the 1930s, Sovietization was largely a project of Russification, with Russian culture and language promoted as the core of Soviet identity. Similar to other national institutions with a religious basis, Jewish, i.e. Yiddish-language schools were closed and religious practices were ousted from the public sphere. If these religious practices continued at all, they were performed in secrecy. At the same time, many younger Jews born after the establishment of the Soviet Union ceased to value their Jewish identity and developed a strong sense of Soviet, civic identity in which their ethnic origin ceased to carry existential meaning in daily life.

In Germany, meanwhile, the Nazi Party (NSDAP) had been elected to government in 1933 and was in the process of transforming and radicalizing German society into a racist state purged of political dissent and national and social groups deemed inimical to German "Aryan" superiority: Jews, Roma, people with disabilities, gays and lesbians, and many others. Shortly after the Nazi rise to power, laws restricting the lives of German Jews were put in place, limiting their ability to work, receive an education, participate in social and political decision-making, or enjoy public parks and swimming pools.

In 1935, the Nuremberg Laws stripped German Jews of their citizenship, after which Jews had few prospects of surviving by their own means. More than 280,000 of the 600,000 German Jews emigrated in the five years following 1933. The rest were often caught between a lack of funds or visas for travel and the bureaucratic obstacles set by potential countries they wanted to immigrate to. Jews wanting to leave were forced to sell their personal property and pay a significant emigration tax. These policies impoverished prospective emigrants and stranded thousands in Nazi Germany who did not have the financial means to leave or were too old to start a life from scratch elsewhere.

As the Nazi government began its aggressive campaign to bring Europe under direct German rule, emigration became less and less feasible. The annexations of Austria and Sudetenland (the northwestern area of Czechoslovakia) in 1938, and finally the attack on Poland in September 1939, created an environment in which the crossing of international borders was nearly impossible. The remaining roughly 200,000 Jews in Germany were doomed to join the Jews in other occupied countries who were singled out, exploited and, finally, killed.

Nazi ideology further posited Bolshevism as the arch-enemy of Aryan Germany. Jews were conceptualized as the personification and promoters of Bolshevik power, and the spectre of Judeo-Bolshevism loomed large in Nazi propaganda that called for the destruction of the Communist state. The public articulation of Nazi ideology was accompanied by active planning for a war to expand into Eastern

Europe and the Soviet Union by politicians, scientists and military strategists. In these plans, the lands to the East were viewed as the living space necessary for German Aryans to prosper. The so-called Generalplan Ost (General Plan East) conceptualized the eastern territories as living space for ethnic Germans and a source of raw materials, its inhabitants to be either exploited as labourers or exterminated as superfluous population, with a distinction drawn between the "low races" of Slavic people and Jews.

In essence, Jews in Germany and the Soviet Union were subject to diametrically opposed agendas and conditions: Nazi ideology singled out Jews based on a racialized understanding of difference and denied Jews their existence as social, political and legal subjects, cumulating eventually in their physical destruction. In the Soviet Union, the reality was much more complicated. Jews, at least in theory, were integrated into society, although it was at the cost of disavowing their Jewish identity and adopting central values of Soviet ideology such as internationalism, secularism and communism. Soviet ideology purported to promote equality and social relationships shaped by conscious and deliberate choice and agency; Nazi ideology, in contrast, was driven by the self-serving notions of superiority that underlie racism and justify the elimination of specific groups.

The inglorious alliance between Nazi Germany and the Soviet government, exemplified by the Treaty of Non-Aggression Pact between Germany and the Soviet Union (Molotov-Ribbentrop pact, 1939) was negotiated during the heated period leading up to the war. On the one side were Allied attempts to curtail Nazi Germany's lust for power without active intervention; economic crisis and demand for heavy and military machinery in the Soviet Union; on the other were Germany's preparation for war and need for raw materials. The Secret Protocols attached to the treaty, which already identified German and Soviet "spheres of influence," didn't become public until 1946 and their existence was denied by the Soviet government until 1989. The Protocols effectively assigned Finland, Estonia, Latvia, Lithuania, and eastern Poland to the Soviet Union, and East Prussia and western Poland to Germany – divisions that were to be implemented through war and the violent overthrow of local regimes.

Germany attacked Poland on September 1, 1939, and the Soviet army began their occupation of Poland later that month. In quick succession, parts of Finland, Estonia, Latvia, Lithuania, Bessarabia, and the northern Bukovina were annexed and incorporated into the Soviet Union. Nieśwież, like many other shtetls and cities with large Jewish populations in the former Pale of Settlement, also fell under Soviet rule; in total, approximately 1.5 million Jews in eastern Poland found themselves living within Soviet borders. For the time being, for the Jews this primarily meant catching up with the Soviet policies of secularization and Sovietization. The *kehilla* was dismantled; Jewish political movements and parties ceased to function; Jewish worker unions were merged with their Polish, Belorussian and Ukrainian counterparts; and many private businesses were closed. The anti-religious campaigning and promotion of Soviet ideology were implemented much faster than in the territories of the USSR as defined in 1922 – a process that had taken almost twenty years in places like Bobruisk in eastern Belorussia was enforced within weeks in the newly annexed parts of Belorussia. Whereas communal Jewish life in pre-war Poland could exist within the framework of Jewish schools, synagogues and self-administration but individual Jews often experienced discrimination, now the opposite was the case: Jews as individuals were, at least on paper, protected by legislation against national hatred and hostility, but the infrastructure of Jewish congregations and communities disappeared.

Simultaneously, many Jews in Poland fled from the newly German-occupied areas. Aware of the discrimination and violence with which the Nazi government and German society had threatened both individual and collective Jewish existence in Germany, more than 400,000 Polish Jews from western and central Poland fled eastward. Some of them soon returned since they saw no prospects for themselves in the Soviet Union or were unable to reunite with their families. Others, like Kutz's mother, who was accused of anti-Soviet activity despite her work with socialist organizations, fell victim to Soviet attempts to eradicate the bourgeois presence or preemptively quell political dissent by activists who supported the Soviet project but criticized particular elements of Soviet policies. They were arrested, thousands of them being deported further inland to Siberia and the far eastern parts of the USSR.

Approximately 100,000 Jews originally from Poland stayed in the Belorussian Republic. Nieśwież's Jewish community grew by about five hundred members. The children, elderly, men and women had to be housed, find work and be integrated into a new environment, a challenge that many towns and cities mastered rather well considering the circumstances of war, ongoing economic crisis, and internal political conflicts within the Soviet Union such as intra-Party strife or debates about the right course to establish a communist society. These refugees, however, also now reported that German atrocities against Polish Jews had begun immediately after the invasion. The spectre of violence loomed over Kutz, his family and Nieśwież's Jews.

The Soviet government had downplayed the threat of war that Nazi Germany posed to the USSR, neglecting to equip the Soviet army with sufficient fuel and ammunition or preparing other means of protecting the population. The German invasion and air raids that began on June 22, 1941 caught both civilians and military by surprise. About two million Soviet combatants were captured in the summer of 1941. Many other Soviet soldiers who escaped turned into guerrilla fighters behind the front line, forming the core of the Soviet partisan movement that became an important element of the military victory against the Nazi regime and of Soviet civilians' struggle for survival.

As German plans to establish a new racial, economic and political order in Europe unfolded, Belorussians, like others in the Soviet Union who fell under the occupation regime, suffered intense violence and hardship: 380,000 residents of Belorussia were deported for forced labour in concentration camps or in Germany; food was requisitioned for the German war effort, causing widespread starvation; and up to 2.3 million residents (25 per cent of the pre-war population) were killed during the war. More than four hundred Belorussian villages were severely damaged or destroyed; another 186 have not been rebuilt since the war. Exploitation and violence, often lethal, targeted the whole Soviet population, but Jews were targeted and subjected to increased humiliation, violation and systematic murder.

Overall, approximately 2.6 million Jews residing in Soviet territories were caught during the German occupation. Within weeks, Communist functionaries and individual Jews, many of them women and men who were part of the Soviet administrative or professional elite, were killed. Beginning in July, Jews in most Belorussian towns were confined to "Jewish residential districts" – i.e., ghettos. Many of these, as in Nieśwież, consisted of a few houses, sometimes even one house, in a specific neighbourhood in which all Jews of a given locality were to reside. Curfews, mandatory wearing of yellow circles or stars, or armbands, and a forced labour regime determined Jewish life under German occupation.

Ghettoization inhibited free access to food and other necessities, fulfilling the German occupation regime's central goal of forcing starvation upon the Jewish population so as to decimate it. Life in the Nazi ghettos in the Soviet Union faced particular difficulties because the Jewish institutions that could have facilitated collective self-help had been destroyed during the anti-religious campaigns in the 1920s and in the course of a reversal in Soviet nationality policies in the 1930s. Michael Kutz and many other youths took on an important role in supplying their families, and themselves, with food: they were highly mobile within the ghettos and also managed to sneak through ghetto fences to barter for or retrieve food outside.

Above all, however, hovered the threat of mass murder. Beginning in late summer of 1941, the Jewish communities between Minsk and

Borisov were annihilated in a concerted campaign of murder sometimes referred to as the "Holocaust by bullets." Nazi killing squads
called Einsatzgruppen, together with collaborating police formations
comprised of locals, Lithuanians, Latvians and Ukrainians, began
mass shootings in ghettos throughout Eastern Europe. When the
Jews of Nieśwież were gathered for execution in late October 1941,
Michael Kutz was separated from his parents and his siblings. The
anguish and despair is palpable in the older Kutz's memoir, as he re-
lates what it meant for him as a young boy to lose the people closest
to him in such a violent atrocity and the connection to a whole world
of learning, caring and planning for the future. Kutz barely escaped
the killing of 4,000 people on that day.

Like a few thousand other children and youth who escaped the
murder in Belorussia, Kutz found shelter with friendly locals before
joining a group of other ghetto refugees who became part of the
Soviet partisan movement. As Jews, however, they faced hostility not
only from local residents, but also from many Soviet partisans, mostly former members of the Soviet army, who were either suspicious of
any civilian who wanted to join them or harboured sometimes violent anti-Jewish attitudes. As a young boy of eleven, Michael was in
an especially precarious position. Like many others in his situation,
he matured quickly and was eventually accepted into the ranks of the
fighters. His experiences are at once characteristic and singular.

Many Jews who managed to escape from the ghettos or flee from
the killing squads tried to join partisan units, knowing this would be
their only chance to survive. Many were denied admission or even
killed. In response to these events, several Jews established their own
Jewish partisan detachments. Lev Gil'chik, Kirill Orlovskii, Boris
Gindin, Israel Lapidus, Pavel Proniagin, Hirsch Kaplinsky and many
others whose name we may never know, commandeered groups of
Jews who decided to wage their own battle against the German occupiers. Eventually, they all joined loosely together in a partisan movement of about 380,000 in Belorussia alone. Among these, it is esti-

mated, were up to 14,000 Jews; in the occupied Soviet Union overall were 35,400 Jewish partisans.

Kutz's memoir also offers insights into two other important elements of the struggle for survival against the Nazi genocide. Hundreds of Jewish children, elderly, women, and men who did not find entry into partisan detachments nevertheless engaged in combat and sabotage missions. They survived in Jewish "family units" such as the detachments led by Tuvia Bielski or Shalom Zorin, who both headed groups of several hundred Jews hiding and surviving in the forests of Belorussia who provided food, clothes, ammunition, medical aid and other necessary services to other partisans and thus secured their own survival. Between 6,500 and 9,000 people lived in such units throughout the occupied Soviet Union; in Belorussia alone there were between 3,700 and 5,200 members.

While the member of a partisan unit, Kutz also learned about the end of Nieśwież' Jewish community: in the summer of 1942, German troops had assembled and killed the remaining five hundred Jews interned in Nieśwież' ghetto. As would happen later on in such towns as Slonim, Kopyl, Mir, Kamenets, Bialystok, Glubokoe, Novogrudok, Kobrin, Liachovichi and Derechin, a group of about thirty people had done what they could to make this destruction as difficult as possible for the Germans. Their efforts had a symbolic character, showing the will to fight the intruder while knowing it to be in vain. This attempt at preserving Jewish honour did produce a concrete result, however, since the fighting enabled several Jews to escape the ghetto and join the partisan movement. In recounting these efforts in the Nieśwież ghetto, Michael Kutz illuminates an aspect of Jewish resistance that we know too little about.

Michael Kutz describes for us the nearly hopeless situation experienced by the Jews residing in German-occupied Belorussia. For Jews who faced a rapidly executed policy of destruction and murder, who were caught behind the front lines, and who, for the most part, could not rely on pre-existing structures of self-help or self-defense, the woods offered the only space to escape from genocide.

All too many Jewish children, women, men, and elderly were not successful in doing so. When Kutz discovered, at the end of the war, that nearly the whole Jewish community of Nieśwież had been annihilated, he shared the realization of many across Belorussia: up to 800,000 Belorussian Jews had been killed by the German occupation regime and its auxiliaries. The centuries-long history of Jews in the Pale of Settlement, Poland and the Soviet Union came to an end.

The teenage Michael Kutz's decision to leave this region was therefore understandable. He had lost his whole family and there was hardly anyone left with whom he could rebuild a life. The second half of his memoir is devoted to the post-war period, beginning with a description of his attempts to reach Israel, an account of his efforts to build a new life in Canada and the emotion he felt when he finally stood at the Holy Wall in Jerusalem.

Kutz provides moving insights into the long and excruciating period of insecurity and waiting that up to ten million displaced people in Europe shared as they waited to repatriate or relocate after World War II, among them former concentration camp inmates, forced labourers, war refugees and prisoners of war. In particular, many of the 250,000 Jewish displaced persons who were unwilling to or incapable of returning to their former hometowns longed for a state that would provide them with security and stability. They were forced to remain in limbo, caught up in the international debate about the formation of a Jewish state and international responsibility for the survivors of the Nazi genocide.

Michael Kutz's account of the decades following the war testifies to a busy life and his work to support marginalized social groups. In some way, these attempts may be understood as an effort to revive the values and forms of mutual assistance that Kutz and his ancestors experienced within the Jewish community of Nieśwież.

Rather than being a memoir of destruction and redemption that results in closure, the following pages are a testimony to the long-lasting impact of the Nazi genocide on a young life. What follows is a rich account of a complicated life that encompasses growing up in interwar Poland, living under Soviet rule, surviving under German occupation and immigrating to Canada. At the same time, Michael Kutz successfully challenges the all-too-common portrayal of the Holocaust as the only salient experience of his and other survivors' lives. As Kutz articulates clearly in these pages, the period of unquestionable traumatization, displacement and loss is not the only important experience in his life.

Anika Walke
Washington University, St. Louis
2013

SOURCES

Ruva Andrusev, Interview 23186, Visual History Archive, usc Shoah Foundation, accessed online at the United States Holocaust Memorial Museum on March 1, 2013.

Yitzhak Arad. *The Holocaust in the Soviet Union*. Lincoln: University of Nebraska Press, 2009.

Yitzhak Arad. *In the Shadow of the Red Banner: Soviet Jews in the War against Nazi Germany*. New York/Jerusalem: Gefen, 2010.

Marat Botvinnik. *Pamiatniki Genotsida Evreev Belarusi*. Minsk: Belaruskaia Navuka, 2000.

Norman Davies and Antony Polonsky (eds). *Jews in Eastern Poland and the ussr, 1939–46*. New York: St. Martin's Press, 1991.

Encyclopedia of Camps and Ghettos, 1933–1945, Vol. II, ed. Martin Dean. Indiana University Press, 2011.

Inna Gerasimova, "Evrei v Partizanskom Dvizhenii Belorussii, 1941–1944: Obshchaia Kharakteristika," *Uroki Kholokosta*, sost. Iakov Z. Basin. Minsk: Kovcheg, 2004.

Christian Gerlach. *Kalkulierte Morde: Die deutsche Wirtschafts- und Vernichtungspolitik in Weißrussland, 1941–1944*. Hamburg: Hamburger Edition 1999.

Michael Marrus. *The Unwanted: European Refugees from the First World War Through the Cold War*. Philadelphia: Temple University Press, 2002 (2nd ed.)

Ezra Mendelsohn. *The Jews of East Central Europe between the World Wars*. Bloomington: Indiana University Press, 1983.

Mikhail Strelets. "Uchastie Evreev v Antigermanskom Soprotivlenii na Okkupirovannoi Territorii Belorussii," *Uroki Kholokosta: Istoria i Sovremennost'*, sost. Iakov Z. Basin. Minsk: Kovcheg, 2004.

Nechama Tec. *Defiance: The Bielski Partisans*. New York: Oxford University Press, 1993.

I dedicate this book to the memory of my family who perished in the Holocaust and especially to my mother, whose vision and faith gave me the courage and determination to survive.

Author's Preface

I will always remember my mother's last words to me. "If, by miracle, you survive, you must bear witness and tell the free world what happened to us." I am the only survivor of the Holocaust from my mother's large family, which originally comprised more than 150 people. Among the few survivors on my father's side were his younger brother, Shimon, the only survivor of seven brothers, and a few of his cousins. That was all that remained of our family.

I often asked myself whether there could be a God who allowed the murder of my family and my people, young and old. When I was ten years old, I heard the last cries of Jews reciting the prayer *Shema Yisrael* on their way to mass graves in my hometown of Nieśwież. As a child, I was angry and disappointed that God had permitted this to happen, but to adopt a negative opinion of God would have meant giving up the struggle to survive and especially giving up on my mother's last words to me. I came to the conclusion that there was a God and that He would give me the determination to live and be free again, and to avenge the Jewish people. I remembered what I had learned in Hebrew school about the two-thousand-year history of our people – how we had survived pogroms, slaughters and inquisitions.

When I was older, I always held on to my mother's words and I promised myself that I would fulfill her wishes by telling Jewish and non-Jewish youth, as well as adults, about everything that our people had been forced to endure during the war, to implore them to pass on our history to future generations so that these events would never happen again.

The Lost Jewish History
of Nieśwież

I was born in the town of Nieśwież, in what is now Belarus, on November 21, 1930. The town is about one hundred kilometres southwest of Minsk and thirty-five kilometres northwest of Kapyl, where the world-famous Yiddish writer Mendele Mocher Sforim was born.[1] The history of the region is long and complex – Nieśwież was founded in the thirteenth century and changed hands many times.

During the eighteenth century, the *szlachta*, the Polish aristocracy, controlled the area and fought against Russia's attempts to occupy it. Ultimately, however, they failed and by the end of the century, Poland, partitioned between Russia, Prussia and Austria, ceased to exist. In the Russian sector in 1794, the Russian empress Catherine the Great suppressed a Polish uprising, as did Tsar Nicholas I in 1830. In 1864, Tsar Alexander II crushed the last of the Polish opposition. From then until 1915, the tsars and their armies ruled Nieśwież and the town was plagued by hunger, typhus and cholera. The Jewish population, just over 3,000 at the time, was subjected to hefty taxes and were the vic-

---

1   For information on Mendele Mocher Sforim, as well as on other people and significant historical events; major organizations; geographical locations; religious and cultural terms; and foreign-language words and expressions contained in the text, please see the glossary.

tims of pogroms – people set fire to the houses where Jews lived. All these misfortunes left the Jewish population impoverished.

In 1919, after World War I, Nieśwież was returned to the newly reconstituted nation of Poland and named a county in the province of Nowogródzkie Województwo. Although people in our town spoke four languages – Polish, Russian, Belorussian and Yiddish, which was the most common – Polish became the official language. The Polish government assumed control and granted Jews the same freedoms that Christians enjoyed; for example, Jews were allowed either to build their own educational institutions to send their children to Polish schools. The Polish authorities, however, didn't trust the majority Belorussian population in the region, and began to assimilate Belorussian Christians into Polish culture. In the early 1920s, the Belorussian language was still taught, albeit barely, but by the 1930s Belorussian children were forced to attend Polish schools and Belorussian books, newspapers and other periodicals were banned from the libraries. The Belorussian Orthodox religion and churches, however, were allowed. It was neither possible nor desirable to completely suppress the Belorussian population because the border to the Belorussian Soviet Socialist Republic, with its powerful Red Army, was only about ten kilometres away.

In 1934, in a further effort to suppress suspected opponents of the Polish regime, the government sent people – including some from our town – to Bereza Kartuska, a concentration camp for political prisoners located a couple of hundred kilometres from Nieśwież, between Pinsk and Sarny. Escape from Bereza Kartuska was impossible, surrounded as it was by the swamps of Polesia. Among the prisoners, which included a large percentage of Ukrainians, were Jews who had been accused of being Communist or Socialist sympathizers. They were considered "undesirable elements" who threatened the existence of the Republic of Poland.

The combination of the earlier unrest in tsarist Russia along with the rise of both the Zionist movement and the socialist movement called the General Jewish Labour Bund had a great impact on the philosophies of Jewish youth in our town. The many active Zionist organizations in Nieśwież included the General Zionists, Mizrachi, Hashomer Hatzair, Gordonia, Poalei Zion, and the Revisionists, including the Betar youth movement. Until 1939, Nieśwież had a Zionist *hachshara* kibbutz, a place where youth spent two years receiving training, especially in agriculture, to prepare for immigrating to British Mandate Palestine. There, they would become part of the kibbutz movement, building up the country for themselves and their children.

During my childhood, Nieśwież had a Zionist Hebrew school and a Yiddish *folkshul* (elementary school) on Michalechok Street, where a lot of working-class Jews lived, a yeshiva and a wonderful library where one could read Hebrew books and journals from all over the world. Students from other towns came to study at the Polish *Gymnasium* (high school) in Nieśwież because universities always accepted students who graduated from there. Local Jewish children studied there as well because their parents believed that higher education would make their children's lives easier than theirs had been.

Nieśwież also had four cheders – religious elementary schools – and fourteen synagogues. I have fond memories of the Kalte synagogue, the largest one in town. At its centre was a grand bimah, a platform covered by a canopy that looked like a chuppah – the traditional wedding canopy – from which hung little silver bells and Stars of David. Across from the bimah and up several steps stood the *aron-koydesh*, the Holy Ark, where the Torah scrolls were kept; it was decorated with the most beautiful gold embroidery. The eternal lamp hung from the high ceiling on a long, golden chain, and in the centre of the ceiling was the painting of a large fish holding its own tail in its mouth. Adults told us that if this fish, the Leviathan, were to let go of its tail, the world would be flooded. When I was young, I spent many sleepless nights afraid of what might happen to everyone. The adults also told us that there were demons in the synagogue at night and if children were to pass by alone, the demons would drag them inside and carry them off to swamps from which they would never return. Whenever I passed by the synagogue after dark, I was so afraid of what might happen to me that I ran as fast as I possibly could.

Our chief rabbi was the head of the *beis din*, the rabbinical court, and represented many of the Jews from the surrounding areas. We also had a well-respected Jewish community council with twelve elected members representing every Jewish organization. I remember that Yoel Rozovsky was president for a long time and that Mr. Yashinovsky was the council secretary. These cultural leaders were connected to Jewish leaders in larger communities and often invited speakers from Warsaw and other cities to lecture about Zionism and the situation for Jews in Europe.

When I was growing up, Nieśwież's Jewish population was about 4,500, which was 60 per cent of the total population. The Jews in the town were mostly tradesmen – hard-working people who exhausted themselves trying to eke out a living for their families. To better their situation, they created a local union and eventually their working conditions improved a great deal. Other Jews in our town practiced a wide variety of professions in the pharmacy, hospital, emergency services, medical clinics and dental offices – I particularly remember the surgeon Dr. Litckowsky, doctors Yacob Ginsburg and Lola Segalowicz, who were loved and esteemed by the entire population, and the dentists Dr. Benjoma-Aizenbid and Nachman Kagan. Mr. Messita, the Jewish lawyer, and Mr. Poliwoda, the Christian lawyer, were among the top jurists in the province. Boruch Shapiro was the chief of our fire station, which had a volunteer brigade of firefighters with fine uniforms, shiny metal hats and its own brass band conducted by a young Jewish man named Pesach Bursky. And how could a town exist without its *royfe*, the old-fashioned self-trained doctor? Moishe the Royfe, as we called him, was a man with a warm heart who would make house calls day and night, foregoing any payment from the poor. Both Jews and Christians adored him.

Jews who were quite poor arrived in Nieśwież on an almost daily basis. The Jewish community built a house for them not far from the synagogue called a *hekdesh*, or poorhouse, where they were given a place to sleep for the night, food, and warm coats, shoes or boots, all donated by the townsfolk. The *hekdesh* was always full of both travellers and the poor. I remember my maternal grandmother, Mariasha, bringing me with her when she delivered warm cooked food and old clothing there. Nieśwież also had a *g'milas chasodim*, a free loan society, where Jews could borrow money to help them build a house or open a small business as long as two townspeople acted as guarantors for the loan. Our *chevra kadisha*, the burial society, was led by religious establishments and operated the funeral home located near the synagogues. They, too, administered to the needs of the poor free of charge, covering the costs of burial and erecting gravestones.

Each spring, a few weeks before Passover, the Jewish community council opened a matzah bakery. The workers, all volunteers, baked enough matzah for the town as well as the nearby villages. People in our community also campaigned outside our community to ask for help in supplying Passover food to impoverished Jewish families. The Nieśwież *Hilfsverein*, or aid society, in New York often helped out the Jewish community by providing funds for its various needs. The members of this group, who had lived in Nieśwież before immigrating to New York, contributed a great deal toward the construction of a building for a new library and also provided money so that children from poor families had milk to drink at school every day.

In the summers, through the ongoing generosity of our community, poor Jewish children in our town were able to attend camp free of charge. The TOZ (Towarzystwo Ochrony Zdrowia Ludności Żydowskiej, or Society for Safeguarding the Health of the Jewish Population) set up a summer camp for Jewish children to learn about nature and enjoy the fresh air. The camp was located six kilometres from Nieśwież in the Mestiansky forest. Every summer, I left town with other children to spend a month participating in activities like hiking deep into the woods and learning how to use a compass to find our way back. We also played football, did gymnastics and learned how to draw. We all came home in good physical condition, with rosy cheeks. I often took part in the other athletic activities offered in our town through the Maccabi sports club, which had both a soccer team and a handball team.

In the fall, on Simchat Torah, my family and I went to synagogue for the *hakafot*, the traditional dance with the Torah scrolls, and I held a white-and-blue paper flag with a candle stuck in an apple on top. Afterward, cakes and cookies were distributed to all the children.

In winter, some of the people in our town could afford to pay my mother's second cousins Yankl and David Zaturensky – who were known as the water-carrier brothers – to bring them water by horse and sleigh, but I remember getting our drinking water from the public wells in town. The closest one to our house was near the market across from the high school. It was difficult to get to the well in winter because of the ice that formed around it; people often slipped and broke an arm or leg. Sometimes the hand pumps would freeze as well, so we would hold some burning straw near the pump to melt the ice. All the children liked to go to the well because it gave us the opportunity to use our skates, which we tied to our winter shoes or boots with string. We skated by the well because none of our parents allowed us to skate on the nearby lake by ourselves. The ice there was not always sufficiently frozen and children sometimes fell through the ice and drowned.

In December, when Chanukah arrived, I remember lighting the coloured candles on the menorah. Everyone sang Chanukah songs and played with *dreydls*, ate hot latkes (potato pancakes) and received Chanukah gelt (coins) from family members. My father would tell my siblings and me about the holiday and recount the heroic struggle of the Jewish fighters. On Purim, the holiday that followed a few months later, we children would go with our older brothers to storekeepers' courtyards to collect wooden boxes. On Purim eve, we took these boxes with us when we went to the synagogues to hear the Megillah, or Book of Esther, and whenever the reader of the Megillah stopped at the name "Haman," who was the villain in the story, we hit the boxes with big sticks as if we were hitting Haman. We made even more noise with our *gragers*, the traditional holiday noisemakers. The *shames* (caretaker) of the synagogue always chased us out and called us *paskudnyaks*, little rascals, but five minutes later we'd be back inside again doing the same thing. The synagogue's warden, as well as members of our community, were on our side and let us continue to "hit" Haman. The following day, we visited our neighbours and relatives to bring them *shalach-manos*, a gift of food, and they would give us *shalach-manos* in return.

My father, Joseph, played an active part in the Jewish community, devoting much of his time to its needs, and my mother, Ida, was a librarian and an active member of a socialist movement in her youth. My father was born in the town of Berezna, Volhynia, part of the Russian Empire at the time, but during World War I he was stationed with the Red Army in Nieśwież, about five hundred kilometres from his hometown. When the war was over, he was demobilized in Nieśwież, where he met and married my mother, Ida Zaturensky, who was born there.

My father worked as a forest broker, assessing the cost of lumber to sell to out-of-town merchants. Every Friday, the end of the work week, my father would take me to the Jewish bathhouse for its *mikvah*, the ritual bath. Then I would lie on a wooden bench in a room that was extremely hot while my father used a special broom made of pine to strike my back and legs to help stimulate the nerves. He would then pour cold water over me from a wooden pail. I was as red as a beet by the time we left!

My mother delivered food supplies to the famous Radziwiłł family, which often gave me the opportunity to visit the Radziwiłł Castle when I was growing up. I remember the grandeur of its halls filled with magnificent art, sculpture, carpets and furniture, and the library full of books in various languages, as well as servants who were fluent in both French and Italian. Count Radziwiłł's castle contained six hundred rooms and served as a guesthouse and rest home for foreign royalty and their families.

The Radziwiłł dynasty had begun in the year 1523 when Mikołaj Radziwiłł, a descendant of the Polish royal family, became the ruler of Nieśwież. In 1583, the Radziwiłł Castle was built beside dense forests on the beautiful Usha River. Surrounded by water, it was accessible only by a drawbridge that could be hoisted up with chains in the event of an attack by marauders. The palace has survived invasions and occupations; even the last two world wars have left it intact and undamaged.

In the sixteenth century, Duke Mikołaj Radziwiłł permitted Jews to settle in Nieśwież to make use of their talents as craftsmen, carpenters, smiths, printers, tailors, shoemakers, wheat merchants and lumber dealers and granted them the same rights as gentiles. The Jewish community contributed greatly to the growth of the town, which began to develop not only economically but also culturally. Many years later, the Radziwiłłs, in gratitude to the Jews for their contributions, built the Kalte synagogue and also gave them protection against pogroms. And in those days, when a large part of the Jewish population lived in poverty, Duke Radziwiłł provided them with food and firewood.

∼

I grew up with three siblings – my brother, Tsalia, who was the eldest, and my older sisters Chana and Nechama. Tsalia was tall, with blue eyes and light blond hair. He was six years older than me and attended first the Hebrew school and then, later, the Polish *Gymnasium*. He was an excellent student and his classmates and friends often came over to do their lessons together, where the aroma of my mother's cooking made the house even more pleasant for them. I respected my brother greatly; firstly, because he was the oldest and secondly, because he and his classmates often discussed Zionism and Theodor Herzl, and Palestine and the *halutz* (pioneer) movement. My brother belonged to the Gordonia Zionist youth organization, and it was his dream to complete two years of the *hachshara* agricultural training before settling on a kibbutz in Eretz Yisrael, the Land of Israel, to help build a Jewish homeland for himself and for future generations.

My sister Chana, who was four years older than me, was a beautiful young girl with brown eyes and dark hair. She attended the *folkshul* and, like my brother, was an excellent student. She played the piano, loved poetry and excelled at drawing. When my parents went out for the evening, she would read me the stories of Robinson Crusoe and Captain Grant as well as fables by the poet Ivan Krylov.

My other sister, Nechama, was two years older than me. She had black curly hair, dark eyes and rosy cheeks. She was also a pupil in the *folkshul*. My mother took her to a ballet studio for lessons twice a week and was always sewing ballet costumes with white crinolines for her. My parents even travelled fifty kilometres to the large city of Baranovichi to purchase her ballet slippers. Nechama often took part in the performances at her school and I was always excited to see her standing on the tips of her toes. She looked like a little angel.

In 1935, when it came time for me to go to school, my parents disagreed over which school I should attend. My father wanted to send me to a secular Hebrew school and my mother wanted me to attend the Yiddish *folkshul*, as my sisters did, where the well-known teacher Mr. Zaltzman, who was also the headmaster, imposed very high standards. My mother's wishes prevailed and I attended the *folkshul* and joined their drama group, which was led by my teacher Elia Rozinsky. We presented plays in the town hall, the Ratush, which had been constructed by the Radziwiłłs in 1596. It stood in the centre of town, impressing everyone with its size and architectural beauty. Artists from Vilna and Warsaw were invited to perform there. Dances were also held in the hall, the proceeds from which went to various causes.

Every day on my way home from school, I attended cheder for

two hours to study prayers, Tanach (the Hebrew scriptures), and Chumash – the print version of the Torah. My teacher, Rabbi Shimon, was an elderly Jew with a white beard who wore a long black coat and kept a leather strap hidden beside him. If a boy laughed during class, the rabbi immediately moved him to another seat. If we didn't pay enough attention to our prayer books, he frequently hit us with the leather strap.

One day, by accident, I came to cheder without my *tsitsis*, my fringed garment, and when the rabbi noticed, he yelled at me, calling me a *shegetz* (a derogatory term for a non-Jew) and he hit my face and ears. I leapt out of my seat and ran home crying. As soon as my mother saw me she put cold compresses on my face. When my father came home, my mother told him what had happened; although they were both upset, they decided that I had to return to cheder the next day because they still wanted me to have a proper Jewish education. But I never went back. Instead, I spent those two hours playing outside with other children, far away from my house. When my father discovered that I wasn't going, he asked me where I had been all those days. I looked him straight in the eye and told him that I would never go back to the cheder. In the ensuing discussion between my parents, my mother suggested that I take French lessons instead, since I learned a bit of Hebrew at the *folkshul*. My father eventually agreed. My French teacher, Rachelle Katz, came from Warsaw and held the lessons in my house.

I was also stubborn about going to the town's movie theatre. Mr. Zusman, who managed the theatre, frequently showed Yiddish films but only allowed children over the age of twelve, accompanied by their parents. Although my friends and I were underage, we couldn't stand missing the chance to see a movie, so we would stand beside the theatre windows, wait for them to be opened to allow fresh air into the hall and jump through them. When my father discovered we were doing this, he whipped me with his leather belt. My friends' fathers did the same. Although I had to promise my father that I would never do it again, my friends and I continued to do the exact same thing whenever we wanted to see a movie.

Three kilometres from town, in the Halba district, was a river surrounded by high trees and walking paths. Every Saturday, all the adults and children went there to admire the scenery and take in the fresh air. In the month of May, the air was filled with the scent of lilacs, which in Polish are called *bez*, and we picked bouquets to take home with us. It wasn't all pleasant, though. Sometimes when my friends and I swam in the river we were attacked by gentile boys who threw stones and called us "dirty Jews." We always fought back and after we had beaten them, they would run off to the surrounding fields.

I think that the non-Jewish population often heard sermons in their churches that preached hatred against Jews, who, according to them, had murdered the son of God, Christ the Saviour. They were also apparently told that Jews were very rich and helped each other out without taking any interest in the gentile population. We were used to hearing about these incitements to violence and the frequent antisemitic demonstrations that resulted from them. A substantial part of the Polish population was antisemitic and, prior to the war, some had belonged to an antisemitic political party known as the Endeks, the National Democrats. But for the most part, at least in my town, gentiles and Jews lived side by side peacefully.

I grew up in a home filled with love. My parents ensured that their children were given everything, especially the opportunity to study and to learn what was happening in the broader world. Journals and newspapers were delivered to us daily and I listened to the discussions at home about various world events. Every evening, some of my father's friends and acquaintances would come to our house to hear the Polish-language BBC broadcasts from London on our Philips shortwave radio.

The dark clouds that hung over Europe once Hitler came to power in Germany in 1933 worried my parents and the Jewish community as a whole. I was almost eight years old on that wintry night in

November 1938 when the Nazis in Germany and Austria, together with the Hitler Youth, set fire to synagogues and other Jewish institutions and shops. They burned sacred books, broke windows in Jewish homes and even shot Jews. The following morning, news of the pogrom, known as Kristallnacht, spread through our town. In all the synagogues, prayers were offered for the Jews of Germany and Austria. At my school, principal Zaltzman ordered all the students to assemble in the main hall. He told us what had happened the night before and how the Nazis had justified Kristallnacht. He explained that Herschel Grynszpan, a seventeen-year-old Jewish boy, had shot and killed the assistant to the German ambassador in Paris, Ernst vom Rath. Herschel, who was born to Polish parents in Germany, could not bear the suffering that his family and friends were enduring at the hands of the Nazis – losing their homes and their jobs, as well as being arrested and forced to leave Germany – and he had decided to do something about it. I prayed for Herschel along with the rest of the students.

This experience had a huge impact on all of us. When I arrived home from school my parents tried to calm me down, but the event was etched in my mind. The following Saturday, in all the synagogues of our town, there were speeches about Hitler's campaign, about how he and his supporters had declared war against the Jews of Europe. The powerful German war machine was ready to occupy parts of Europe and execute its anti-Jewish decrees. We all wondered what would happen to us.

Life Under Soviet Rule

In the summer of 1939, the 27th Cavalry Regiment stationed in the Nieśwież barracks, the regiment in which Jewish soldiers and officers from all over Poland served, suddenly left with all its military equipment and set out on the road leading to the forests around Baranovichi. People were frightened by rumours from well-informed sources that Germany was about to attack Poland. After what had happened to Czechoslovakia – with Germany occupying part of the country in the fall of 1938 and invading the rest in the spring of 1939 – anything was possible. My father and his friends continued to listen to the radio broadcasts from London, heatedly debating whether England would come to Poland's aid or leave her to the same tragic fate as Czechoslovakia.

My father was a very liberal man who allowed his children to hear all the news of the world, so my brother, Tsalia, and I sat on the floor and listened to everything. Afterward, when we related what we had heard to our friends, their parents complained to mine, arguing that children shouldn't be allowed to hear such bad news. They were trying, in vain, to protect their children from the terrible events that were taking place.

Late one summer evening near the end of August 1939, we heard the news from London on the shortwave radio that on August 23, Germany and the Soviet Union had concluded a non-aggression pact signed by their foreign ministers, Joachim von Ribbentrop, and Vyacheslav Molotov. The Soviet dictator Joseph Stalin was now an ally and friend of the Hitler regime. Much later, we understood that the Soviet Union was giving Hitler permission to attack Poland, which did not take long to happen. On September 1, 1939, the powerful German army and air force invaded Poland. The Polish army defended the country heroically, but the German Wehrmacht, with its army, navy and air force, swiftly routed the demoralized Polish army and its cavalry, pushing them as far east as the Vistula River, which divided Poland from north to south. Jewish soldiers also bravely fought alongside the Poles but many of them either fell in battle or were captured as prisoners of war (POWs).

The Polish authorities in my town had proclaimed a state of war and young men were drafted into the army, but the mobilization was never realized. Although the British prime minister, Neville Chamberlain, had promised that England would go to war to help Poland in the event of a German attack, that support never materialized. A few weeks later, Poland ceased to exist as an independent country.

On September 17, 1939, according to the terms of the secret pact between the Soviet Union and Germany to divide Poland between them, the Red Army occupied the eastern part of Poland without any resistance. In the eyes of the world, the victorious Red Army had liberated the minority Belorussian population from Polish enslavement. A border was immediately established; on one side was the German army and on the other, the Red Army and its commissars.

The influx of Jews from the German-occupied Polish territories quickly intensified. Refugees had no difficulty crossing the border to the Soviet side since, in many cases, the Red Army turned a blind eye and allowed them to cross. On the Belorussian side of the border, including in Nieśwież, this influx created tremendous problems with housing, which had to be found for the newcomers. Nonetheless, the Jews of our town welcomed them warmly and did what they could to provide assistance. Our family took in Yankl and Manya Gelfand, a Jewish couple from Siedlce. They told us what the Nazis had done to the Jewish population when they invaded Poland. The first to enter the towns and villages were the German army divisions and behind them, on motorcycles, were the Einsatzgruppen and the SS. They were all responsible for attacking Jewish families, raping Jewish women and girls and killing Jews. At the very beginning of the occupation they shot Polish civilians as well, but most of the people they killed were Jews. In some small towns the Nazis shot only the men, leaving women, children and the elderly to fend for themselves. They also shot most of the Jewish intelligentsia and professionals, who had no means of defending themselves. The Nazis and their collaborators burned synagogues and Jewish institutions; Jewish businesses and factories were plundered; and the Nazis stole gold jewellery, silverware, fur coats and warm blankets from Jewish houses. Houses were sometimes set on fire with families inside, prevented from escaping.

That September day in 1939 when the Red Army crossed the previous border that was only a few kilometres from Nieśwież, the tank brigade was the first to enter the town, followed by the artillery with its large cannons, and then by Red Army soldiers on massive trucks. The town was taken without any resistance – there were no Polish soldiers left in the area – and the Red Army took over the former Polish barracks. Their military commissar ordered all men between the ages of seventeen and fifty to present themselves at his headquarters, formerly the headquarters of the Polish county police. A volunteer militia was formed to maintain order in the town and surrounding areas. Most of the volunteers were Belorussian, but some were Jewish. The Jews didn't sign up out of love for the Soviet authorities, but to bring order to the town and help normalize daily life. My father became a volunteer militiaman, wearing a broad red band on his arm and a rifle on his shoulder. My siblings and I found it very strange to have weapons in the house.

In the Red Army there were several Jewish soldiers and high-ranking officers – I remember seeing tanks with Jewish tank drivers sitting on top of them on the main street near the market. One of our neighbours asked one of them, "How is your economic and political situation?" His answer was, "If one lives, one doesn't lack problems." It did not require an expert to understand that.

The Soviet authorities sent hundreds of political commissars into their occupied territories to impose the Soviet system on the population. They closed down houses of prayer and our beautiful main synagogue, the Kalte, was transformed into a lumber warehouse and carpentry workshop to teach young people a trade. All the cheders and Hebrew schools were also shut down, as were the Zionist organizations, and the Bund and the trade unions ceased to exist. The Yiddish theatre, too, was locked up, as was the building housing the Jewish community centre. Everything I had grown up with prior to the occupation was taken over by the Soviet authorities and their bureaucrats.

After all the Jewish institutions in Nieśwież had been closed down, the N K V D, the secret police, began arresting Jews they determined to be "suspect," as well as community leaders. People were arrested for belonging either to a Zionist organization or to the Socialist Bund, and some were then sent with their families to the notorious slave labour camps for political prisoners in Siberia. The deputy mayor of Nieśwież was arrested, as was the chairman of the Jewish community council, Yehuda Levitsky, along with his wife, Freydl. Not all of them returned from their sentences – in 1940, Yoel Rozovsky, who had been president of the council, was shot in a camp in Siberia.

The Red Army also arrested Prince Radziwiłł and his family. They were first held prisoner in Minsk and then imprisoned in the Lubyanka prison in Moscow. After a few months, through pressure from the Italian royal family and Mussolini, the Radziwiłł family was released and allowed to settle in Rome, leaving the castle with all its art and riches for the Soviet authorities. The Radziwiłł dynasty, which had existed in my town for hundreds of years, became a part of history.

In the Yiddish school, which was now a Soviet-Yiddish school, as well as in the Belorussian schools, pupils were forced to join the Young Pioneers, the Communist youth organization. Each of us had to wear the standard uniform, a white shirt and a red tie. The group's leaders lectured us about Stalin, our "great father" who was concerned about our welfare, and about the great future that would be ours. Pioneers were told to be on guard against the enemies of the Fatherland, which meant that if we heard anyone on the street or at home speaking against our country or Father Stalin, we were to inform our leaders immediately. Parents were afraid to talk about the Soviet system at home because children had reported these conversations to their Pioneer leaders. You can imagine what happened to their parents when the notorious NKVD knocked on their door late at night.

The older youth had to become members of the Komsomol, which was a springboard to later becoming members of the Communist Party. A large part of the population joined the Party simply because a membership card made it easier for them to find work and obtain food and clothing for their families.

The Soviet authorities forced Jewish shops to stay open until their shelves were empty and they nationalized small factories and private workshops, ordering the owners to work under the direction of the Commissariat. Our townspeople soon felt the shortage of food, clothing and housing. The warehouses belonging to the authorities were mostly empty, but vodka was still available. The black market, with its high prices, flourished. Whenever the town militia arrested a *spekulant* – someone who sold goods for profit – all the goods in his or her possession were confiscated and the person was sentenced to jail without a trial. The shortest sentence was five years. A joke started making the rounds that whoever had not been in jail would be, and whoever had already been in jail would never forget it. Many of the Jews in our town were declared enemies of the state; some even hanged themselves to avoid arrest.

The Soviet government particularly did not trust the Jewish refugees from Poland, even accusing them of being spies and supplying information to the Germans on the other side of the border. They were characterized as *spekulanty* who went back and forth across the border trading in gold, currency, jewellery and watches. It was true that some refugees wanted to return to German-occupied territory in order to reunite with the families they had left behind, and older Polish Jews remembered the Germans from World War I as being friendly to the Jews. The Soviets, however, wanted to end all this activity. It did not take long before the government organs posted notices that stated that any Polish Jews wishing to return to their former homes in German-occupied territory had to register to obtain documents giving them permission to leave the territory under Soviet control.

One summer night in 1940, all the Polish Jews who had registered were arrested in their homes. The government and the NKVD had devised a secret plan and prepared train cars in designated stations. Instead of returning to Poland, their now-prisoners, who were allowed to bring only one small suitcase, were taken in trucks to the designated stations and sent to labour camps in Siberia. There is a Yiddish saying that when you're unlucky, you still need luck. As it turned out, many of them were fortunate to have been sent to the labour camps in Siberia, where they survived, instead of facing certain death at the hands of the Nazis and their collaborators. Some Polish Jews sent to Siberia, however, still died from hunger, disease and the harsh living conditions under the northern Soviet regime.

Much later, after Germany suddenly attacked the Soviet Union at the end of June 1941, the Polish government-in-exile made a treaty with the Soviet government that freed all Polish citizens in the Siberian labour camps. When they were liberated, they were given permission to settle in cities such as Tashkent and Samarkand in Uzbekistan, and Alma-Ata in Kazakhstan.

One of the Jews freed from the camps in Siberia was the legendary hero Menachem Begin, who became leader of the Irgun, the Jewish paramilitary force in British Mandate Palestine, and, many years later, prime minister of Israel. Along with other Jewish men, Begin enlisted in the Polish army-in-exile, organized by General Sikorski to fight against Nazi Germany. Led by Władysław Anders, this force became known as Anders' Army. It was through the army that Begin reached Palestine to eventually become commander of the Irgun and fight against British rule.

Later, in 1943, Jews were also recruited into the Soviet-organized First Polish Army through the efforts of Wanda Wasilewska, who was president of the Union of Polish Patriots, a Soviet-led communist organization. These divisions fought under the leadership of the Red Army, whose heroic general, Marshal Zhukov, freed most of Poland.

~

In December 1940, in the middle of the night, the NKVD knocked on our door. We all woke up to see three men armed with rifles. They ordered my mother to dress quickly and, without telling her what crime she was accused of, took her to the town jail. Early the next day my father went to see the commandant of the jail to ask why she had been arrested. In response, the commandant showed my father a list that "proved" that my mother had once belonged to the socialist movement; the document indicated that she had signed a petition in the late 1930s protesting the shooting death of commissars Zinoviev and Kamenev, and, in a separate incident, commissar Blyukher, all victims of Stalin's purges. My mother was not put on trial – NKVD procedure was to force the arrested person to voluntarily confess to their supposed crime. That night, my mother was taken from her cell and pressured to sign a confession but she refused to sign anything that declared she was guilty.

The night after my mother's arrest, my father and Tsalia dug a hole in our yard to bury all her books connected to anti-Soviet activities. The earth was already frozen at that time, so it was only with great effort that they succeeded in digging the hole. Once the hole was covered, they poured water over it, allowed it to freeze, and then added a layer of snow. Our home was now purged of "undesirable" literature.

Once a week, my father took me to visit my mother and bring her food and clean clothing. Some young Jewish men working as guards in the jail helped my father by giving him more opportunities to visit my mother and make her life there a little more comfortable. After four long, difficult months my mother was released, but her Soviet passport was not returned to her.

Tragedy

On June 22, 1941, Germany invaded the Soviet Union. That morning, we heard the loud rumble of tanks and everyone streamed into the streets to see what was happening. We saw columns of trucks heading for the road that led to the Gorodeya train station on the rail line to Baranovichi and Brest-Litovsk, where the front line was located at that time: the Red Army soldiers were leaving town.

In a massive panic, Soviet citizens who had played a role in the Soviet administration also attempted to leave. However, because the Soviet commissars had already seized all the horses and wagons to take themselves to the train station, it was impossible for these people and their families to find transportation. They had to set out on foot toward the town of Slutsk on the 1939 border and then try to reach the city of Minsk, one hundred kilometres away. A small number of them did reach Minsk – although it too was soon invaded by German paratroopers – but the majority, travelling with families and small children, were forced to return to Nieśwież. When the German army occupied Nieśwież, these Soviet citizens were their first victims.

The Red Army was still retreating from the advancing German army two days later. Some Soviet soldiers came through town in trucks but most were on foot. The Germans soon started to fire on Nieśwież and by Saturday evening, June 28, my town was occupied. That same evening, German SA soldiers in brown uniforms with red swastikas on the sleeves patrolled the town and its surroundings on motorcycles.

The next morning, Belorussians began looting the Soviet warehouses, stealing whatever they could. That evening, the German army imposed a curfew and the streets were empty. I remember being at home with my brother and sisters, doors locked and windows closed, afraid that the gentiles were planning a pogrom. My mother was scared too, and often cried; she missed my father, who had been mobilized by the Red Army a few months earlier. His group of soldiers, most of whom were Jews, had been driven to the former Soviet border in the region of Slutsk and Bobruisk. My mother had become the breadwinner, responsible for our day-to-day existence.

A few days later, the new Nazi authorities appointed Magalif as the chairman of the Judenrat, a Jewish council under their control. He was a Polish-Jewish refugee, a lawyer who had come from Warsaw, and he spoke German well. It was extremely difficult to find Jews who were willing to become members of the Judenrat – most of the Jews of Nieśwież did not want to collaborate with the Nazis. Once the Judenrat was established, the commandant of Nieśwież ordered its chairman to organize a Jewish police force. Most of those who volunteered for it were the Polish-Jewish refugees who had fled the 1939 German occupation and settled in Nieśwież.

The Judenrat and the police carried out all the commandant's orders diligently and forced the rest of the Jews to do the same. The first decree, in the early fall, ordered all Jews whose homes were centrally located to move out at once and relocate to the new Jewish section surrounding the courtyard of the Kalte synagogue. This section, now called the ghetto, was very small and was in the neighbourhood that contained the Jewish schools, the cheders and the Talmud Torahs. We already lived in that area, but others were given only four hours to move out of their homes. They were only allowed to take handbags or suitcases, so people wore as many clothes as they could. The rest of their possessions, including furniture, were left behind and confiscated by the Belorussian police, who delivered most of it to the Nazis' barracks. A few days later, certain privileged non-Jews who had voluntarily collaborated with the Nazis moved into the empty houses and robbed other ones. When Jews did find the opportunity to return to the homes they had been forced to abandon, to fetch some of their belongings, they were either beaten up by the new residents or threatened with being handed over to the Nazis. To avoid that fate, they had no choice but to run back to their new homes in the Jewish quarter.

Next, the German commandant ordered the Judenrat to collect fur coats and leather boots from the Jewish population. Then they had to seize all unused men's underwear, woollen sweaters, and new blankets and sheets. An increasing number of items were taken and delivered to the authorities – silver and copper objects, candelabras, goblets, gold, rings, earrings, bracelets, pearls, and paintings by known artists. The Germans sent some of these confiscated items to their families in Germany. To ensure that their orders were enforced, the Nazis would take a group of Jewish men hostage and, if the quotas were not filled, shoot them. The Judenrat went from house to house to collect the requisite items and ensure that they were delivered to Nazi headquarters at the appointed time. Sometimes, Nazi officers went into Jewish homes themselves and confiscated any valuable carpets or pieces of hand-carved furniture.

The authorities had opened transit quarters – temporary housing – for the German infantry and its high-ranking officers that required furniture, beds, linens, cooking pots, dishes and cutlery. The Judenrat had to ensure that these, too, were provided promptly or the entire Jewish community would be held responsible.

The Judenrat then began to register all the Jews in Nieśwież. When the Judenrat presented the list to the German commandant, he ordered them to organize work groups of men, women and even children. Tsalia was the first name on the list of people designated to clean the streets and sidewalks. Although I was only ten years old, I was assigned to clean the public toilets, but Tsalia somehow arranged for me to go with his group. Early each morning, we met near the Judenrat office and marched in single file to clean the streets in the centre of town. I carried a broom in one hand and a shovel in the other. We had to shovel horse manure into canvas bags and then carry the bags on our backs to a dump site.

Our group, which included several other children, did eventually have to clean the public toilets, which the Nazis usually ordered us to do with our hands. They often photographed us doing the work. For the most part, we complied because we just wanted to return home safely to our families – if someone disobeyed a command, they were beaten on the head with rubber truncheons. We also heard more serious warnings from the Nazi authorities that forced labour workers were occasionally shot for disobedience.

To provide the Germans with heat for their lodgings, peasants from the neighbouring villages supplied logs from the forests around Nieśwież. Jewish men and older boys had to cut up the wood and arrange it in neat piles. Tsalia and I were soon placed among the woodcutters. We were escorted on our way to work by the Belorussian police, who watched for Jews trying to escape. My hands got covered in calluses from the work, but it wasn't long before I became used to it.

Jewish girls and women worked at Nazi headquarters doing laundry, ironing shirts and uniforms, cleaning rooms, peeling potatoes and washing pots. They were often raped by the officers. Some of the young women who had belonged to Zionist organizations before the war were trained in the use of machine guns, revolvers and hand grenades, and managed to smuggle out parts of weapons hidden beneath their clothing and deliver them to people in the newly formed Jewish underground resistance. These girls had to be very careful because the police usually searched their backpacks at the end of each day.

With each passing day, hunger became more and more widespread among the Jewish population, and there were instances of sympathetic gentiles selling potatoes and flour to Jews. Whenever the police saw Jews with food supplies, they either arrested them or shot them on the spot and then punished the townspeople for helping them.

My mother used to tell us that necessity is the mother of invention. When we suggested to her that in the evenings, after dark, we could take our clean tablecloths and linen to exchange for food, she, her voice trembling, agreed, choosing me for this task because I was fast and careful. So I became a courier in the dark of night, exchanging these items with non-Jewish acquaintances for bread. I had to assume the responsibilities of an adult, taking the place of our father in the home. My mother and my siblings and I missed him very much, but our lives had to go on without him. It felt as if my childhood had vanished overnight, stolen from me at a time when my friends and I should have been playing outside and going to school. Although I had always hoped that I would learn the Haftorah for my bar mitzvah, I now sensed that this would never happen. I began to understand what was happening around us.

Every day, the Nazis imposed new laws that led to more hardships. The curfew remained in effect; we were forbidden to walk on the sidewalks; and we had to wear white arm bands and a black Star of David over the heart, which was later changed to a yellow Star of David on the right side of the chest and on the back. The Nazis called us names such as *verfluchte Juden* (damned Jews) or *Jüdische Untermenschen* (subhuman Jews). If a Nazi noticed a Jew not wearing a Star of David, he or she would be shot for not following orders. These incidents usually involved the elderly, children or the mentally challenged.

Jews were frequently arrested without knowing why, taken to Gestapo headquarters and shot. The collaborating Belorussian police killed anyone who resisted arrest. I heard that some were tortured and brutally beaten, their heads bashed with pickaxes. Afterward, the commandant would order the Judenrat to bring Jews to remove the bodies and bury them in graves that they had been forced to dig. Another group had to wash the blood from the commandant's courtyard.

Not far from Nieśwież was a village called Glinistcha where Jews who had been caught buying food from gentiles were imprisoned along with Red Army soldiers, Roma (called Gypsies at the time), Jewish Red Army officers and communists. Hundreds of prisoners were killed there every day and early every morning Jewish men were ordered to dig graves for the innocent victims. When the executions were over for the day, prisoners were ordered to cover the graves. We got this news from peasants in the area around Nieśwież, who could hear the screams of those being tortured prior to their execution. They told us that the Roma fought back with their bare hands. We were also told that the Soviet prisoners of war shouted slogans such as, "Long live the Soviet Union!" "Long live the Red Army!" "Our Fatherland will take revenge on you for the bloodshed of our people!" "We will fight and destroy you for all time!"

We were not only aware of what was happening in Glinistcha, but throughout August, September and October we also heard news about mass murders in nearby towns and villages, as well as in bigger cities like Minsk, Slutsk and Pinsk. We felt hopeless and our morale was very low. Every day, we expected the worst.

On October 29, 1941, the chairman of the Judenrat received an announcement from the German commandant of Nieśwież that the *Gebietskommissar* (district commissar) of Baranovichi had ordered all Jews to gather in the market square in the centre of town at 8:00 a.m. the next day, October 30. The Jewish police went from house to house with the militia to inform us that the next day we were to put on clean, warm clothing and bring our passports and birth certificates. We couldn't sleep that night. Everyone in the house sensed that something terrible was about to happen. The neighbours came over and we comforted each other with the thought that perhaps the Germans were sending us to work camps or to a larger ghetto enclosed with barbed wire, something that we'd heard about. Some of us wept and hoped for a miracle.

By 6:30 a.m. the next morning my mother and all of us children were dressed in our best clothes and warm coats. It was cold outside. At 7:00 a.m. the Jewish police went from street to street, ordering people to leave their homes and march to the market square. By 8:00 a.m., we had to be standing in rows with our families. Parents made their way through the streets, some carrying small children in their arms. Older children held their parents' hands. The elderly – grandmothers and grandfathers – many of whom were in poor health, also marched to the market square. Those who were very sick remained bedridden in their homes. I later found out that the Belorussian police searched all the houses that same day and killed anyone who had remained at home.

When my mother, my brother, my two sisters and I arrived at the market square we were put into a row. After the entire Jewish population of the town – about 4,500 people – had assembled in the square, Lithuanians, Ukrainians, Belorussians and the auxiliary police, all with automatic weapons on their shoulders and revolvers on their hips, suddenly appeared on trucks. Most of these murderers – known as the Einsatzgruppen – were drunk and reeked of vodka. Minutes later, these Nazi collaborators, many whose uniforms were already covered in blood, surrounded us. I learned later that they had carried out an earlier *Aktion* in the town of Kletsk, fifteen kilometres from Nieśwież. At 8:00 o'clock sharp the German commandant and several SS officers, one of them a red-headed high-ranking officer, began to carry out their gruesome plan.

First, all the tradesmen and professionals and their families were ordered to stand in separate rows. The commandant had a list of these workers – doctors, engineers, textile workers, carpenters, painters, brick layers, mechanics, tailors, shoemakers – and how many of them there should be. Most of the families were divided because people did not want to leave their elderly grandparents. There were close to six hundred people selected, a very small number of them with their families, and they were separated from the rest of us and ordered to march the short distance to the schoolyard of the Nieśwież *Gymnasium*.

At the square, families were soon separated – children from parents and parents from children. This caused a huge commotion of people shouting and crying. Everyone wanted to run, without knowing where. My mother's last words to me were, "My dear, beloved child. If, by miracle, you survive, you must bear witness. I believe that God will protect you so that you will remain alive to tell the free world what happened to us." My mother pressed me to her and kissed me. Then shots were fired into the air, possibly intending to quiet us, but the situation only worsened. People started pushing and stepping on one another. During the pushing and shoving, I was separated from my family.

The confusion did not last long because the killers soon got the upper hand. They placed us into groups of about one hundred to two hundred people. When it had quieted down, I saw that the Einsatzgruppen had again surrounded us on all sides. No one had any chance of escaping. Almost everyone was crying in despair at being separated from their loved ones. Hopeless, our spirits broken, we stood in line and waited for the order to march. Where we were marching, no one knew, but we all seemed to sense that we were going on our final journey. One group after the other began leaving the square. The first groups went to the left, the others to the right. I saw SS officers photographing us – parents holding small children, older children walking hand in hand with their parents, the elderly holding on to one another.

I felt dejected. With tears in my eyes, I joined a column. My eyes darted in every direction, hoping for a chance to see someone from my family. Tragically, I couldn't see anyone. On the commandant's order, the columns moved forward. My column was at the back, so I was able to see that the ones who were leaving the square were heavily guarded. Although the guards were beating people, there were still individuals who had the courage to run away. They were quickly shot, as a warning to all of us not to try to escape.

The day grew colder. In the cloudy sky high above us I could see birds that had stayed for the winter still flying freely. If only I could fly, I thought, I could escape. Instead, I stood under close surveillance, wondering what was going to become of me. As the order was given for my group to proceed, I suddenly realized where they were taking us – to Count Radziwiłł's castle.

Some young people broke away from our column and started to run, but I immediately heard shots and then saw them fall down. Not far away, the same happened in other groups. I, too, had considered escaping, but walking beside me was a Belorussian policeman with a loaded rifle, ready to shoot. I didn't have an opportunity to even try and make a run for it.

As our column passed under the tall trees of the thickly forested park surrounding the castle, I heard more shots and understood what was happening. There, among the trees, we were stopped and ordered to get completely undressed. Those who did not obey were beaten. Pious bearded Jews and young women covered parts of their bodies with their hands. I heard the cries of children and the prayers of their parents and more shots – the execution of the groups that had preceded ours. When the shots stopped, our group was led forward about 140 metres to open pits that were now mass graves. People were ordered to jump in. I watched the Einsatzgruppen tear tiny infants from their mother's arms, throw them into the air with one hand, and shoot them with the revolver they held in their other hand. When the infants fell to the ground, the Nazis picked up the small bodies and threw them into the pits. The mothers who witnessed this execution of their children threw themselves on the murderers and were shot on the spot. Parents who tried to protect their children with their own bodies were also shot.

As I marched toward the pit I saw some young men trying to attack the Einsatzgruppen with their bare hands. One shouted, "We will take revenge on you for spilling our innocent blood!" They were beaten mercilessly before receiving a bullet to the head. The Nazis photographed the executions and watched the murder of innocents with smiles on their faces.

I clearly remember standing with my back to the pit, facing the murderers. One ran over to me and hit me on the head with his rifle. The next thing I knew, I was inside the pit and at some point, opened my eyes to a horrifying sight. I lay among the dead and dying – there were people under me who were buried alive. I heard the moans of people underneath me and on top of me. Although I was only a child, I somehow found the strength to push the bodies off me and tried to stand up. My head was spinning. My body and face were covered in blood. Realizing that I was not seriously injured, I managed to stand up and look for anyone else around me who was not either dead or fatally wounded. There was no one.

The pit in which I found myself had not yet been covered over. Much later, I found out that this was because the last remaining Jews from the surrounding villages were to be brought here the next morning. When I could no longer hear any shooting, I carefully tried to see what was happening above ground, to check whether the graves were being guarded, but I was too small to see out of the pit. I summoned the strength to drag some of the bodies into a pile and, by climbing up on top of them, was able to stick my head out of the pit. In my mind I could still hear my mother saying, "My dear child, you must survive." I didn't see anyone outside the pit, so I jumped out. Although it was getting dark, I knew the area very well and started running. I had the feeling that my mother was running beside me and calling out to me, "Michael, run faster and don't look back!"

Refuge and Resistance

I ran about two kilometres to a Catholic convent, approached the gate and pulled the bell cord. It didn't take long before a small window in the gate opened and a nun's face appeared. It was the Mother Ksieni, the convent's mother superior. She immediately opened the door and pulled me in; seeing that I was stark naked, she put her black robe around me and led me into a small, windowless room furnished with only a table, a chair and a picture of the Madonna hanging on the wall. She left me alone there for a few minutes, then returned with two nuns and told me to go with them to a bathroom, where they gave me a long towel, hot water and soap to wash the dried blood off my body. Mother Ksieni brought me underwear as well as a large pair of trousers, a pair of slippers and a peasant's coat and hat. All the clothes belonged to the convent's caretaker and were much too big for me, but I put them on. The nuns then offered me something to eat. Although I refused the food, I asked them for a glass of milk.

Mother Ksieni looked sad as she explained that I could not stay for very long because both the German and the Belorussian police were searching the area for escaped Jews. If they were to catch me there, everyone would be shot. I told them that my father was friends with a Polish-Catholic family who lived near the village of Rudawka and that if I could get there, the family would surely hide me. The nuns gave me directions for the five-kilometre trek through forest and fields. As I said goodbye, the nuns and the mother superior knelt down to give me a blessing to help me reach the Polish peasant safely.

It was dark as I walked through the forest. I was afraid of getting lost and kept very close to the fields. When I finally saw a light in the distance, I was careful to make sure that I had found the right house, with its large barn and red tin roof. Because my father had often taken me there, I remembered that the house was half a kilometre from the village and that there was a doghouse in front with a big dog chained to it. As soon as I got close to the barn, the dog started to bark and a man came out of the house, shouting in Polish, "Who's there?" I answered that I was Joseph Kutz's son Michael. My father's friend, Kazimierz, immediately ran over and pulled me into the house, dimmed the kitchen light and woke up his wife. As soon as she saw me, she took me in her arms, began to cry and kissed me. They asked me how I had survived and, when I told them what had happened to me, they confirmed the horrible fate of the rest of the Jews of Nieśwież. They were furious at the collaborators who had participated in the massacre.

Kazimierz and his wife said that they would hide me for the winter and started to plan where I could hide. Then they woke up their three children, a girl and two boys. When the children came into the kitchen and recognized me, their father explained that I was the only one of my entire family to survive. "Your mother and I have decided to hide Michael for the winter," he told them. "No one in school or in the village or in our extended family must know that a Jewish boy is hiding in our house. If anyone finds out, the local police and the Germans will burn down our house and our farm and shoot us all." The father had the children kneel on the floor and swear to Jesus that they would keep this secret. And so it was.

During the day I sat in a windowless attic and in the evening I went into the barn with Kazimierz to feed the cow, the horse, the pigs and the chickens. If a member of their family visited the house, I was hidden in the barn under hay and straw. They were all very good to me; every day they would tell me news about what was happening in our area as well as in the Nieśwież ghetto, where approximately six hundred Jews remained. They also gave me news about what was happening on all the fronts of the war, especially about events around Moscow, where the Red Army had temporarily halted the German advance in the winter of 1941.

My father's friend was also the one who explained why one of the mass graves in the Radziwiłł Park had not been covered up right away. The day after the mass killings in Nieśwież, the Lithuanian Einsatzgruppen had brought corpses from the surrounding villages and thrown them into the pit where I had been. From that time on, the town of Nieśwież and the surrounding villages were almost *judenrein*, the Nazi term meaning cleansed of Jews. Only the Jews in the ghetto remained alive, forced by the Germans and their collaborators to do difficult physical labour while suffering from hunger and disease.

At night, alone in my hiding place, I often woke up crying. Kazimierz and his wife would hear my sobs and come to comfort me. Day and night I thought about my mother, my brother and my sisters, about how they had been shot and where their bodies might be, either near the Snów road in the sand pits about fifteen kilometres from Nieśwież or in the mass graves in Radziwiłł Park. On many sleepless nights I also thought about my father at the front, having left behind the whole family, taking revenge on the German army.

Kazimierz told me that every Sunday in the Catholic church he prayed to God for my safety so that no harm would come to me. He said that we are all children of God and that he would help me to survive this terrible war and once again be free. To help me pass the time in my hiding place, he brought me Russian books by Dostoevsky, Tolstoy, Pushkin and Lermontov, as well as a book, translated into Russian, by Adam Mickiewicz, a famous Polish friend of the Jews. Mickiewicz was born in the nearby town of Nowogródek and had publicly campaigned for equal rights for the Jewish population. Kazimierz apologized that he had no books by Jewish writers – after the massacre of the Jewish population, the Nazis and their Belorussian helpers had taken all the books from Jewish homes, including hundreds of prayer books, and delivered them to the German army. The army accumulated a mountain of books, including historic manuscripts, poured flammable liquid over the pile and set it on fire. The fire and the smoke could apparently be seen from far away.

As there was no window in my hiding place, the sun never shone there, but a kerosene lamp provided me with light to read. I often suffered from headaches because the air was saturated with kerosene, but I accepted everything with gratitude to the family, who had risked their lives to hide me over the winter. My father's friend used to tell me that the Nazis placed no value on Jewish lives. For him, however, saving a Jewish life was like saving his own life. After my liberation, I learned that another Catholic family my father knew, the Zubowiczs, had hidden two Jewish boys from the Rutenberg family along with the lumber merchant Jacob Lifshitz, all of whom were from Nieśwież.

Kazimierz also told me about the Jews in the Nieśwież ghetto who were trying to survive deprivation, hunger and cold. He said that many had not made it through the winter. I learned much more about the Jews in the ghetto after the war – they had moved into some of the houses belonging to people who had been murdered on that day in October. With four families to a house, it was extremely crowded. Each of the survivors had lost some of their family, but they tried to go on. Their food ration consisted of about seventy grams of bread and fifteen grams of meat a day for each person, although they were not always given this amount every day. They were starving, dying from hunger and other illnesses.

A three-metre high barbed wire fence enclosed the ghetto. A high tower had been erected at the entrance to the ghetto, with a small guardhouse for the Jewish police. Their task was to control all entry into and exit from the ghetto. There were workshops inside the ghetto, in the synagogues, for shoemakers, tailors, carpenters and painters.

The rest of the Jews in the ghetto worked in the service of the German headquarters and the commandant. The men cut firewood for them or worked in their gardens in the neighbourhood of Ogrodowa Street. The women cleaned their rooms, washed their toilets, laundered and ironed their underwear and uniforms, and cleaned the streets. All the Jews, young and old, had to work, and Jewish men often had to dig graves for the victims of the Nazis' executions.

Early each morning, Jews who worked outside the ghetto were led out under heavy guard, and then brought back in at night. It was very difficult to smuggle food into the ghetto; if any food, even a piece of bread, was discovered, the punishment was death. Still, some decided to risk their lives by cutting through the barbed wire to exchange their possessions with gentiles for some potatoes or flour and try to smuggle it back in. Some were discovered and killed as they tried to get through the barbed wire fence and others were caught on the outside. People often turned Jews over to the Nazis. As payment, they would receive one kilogram of salt and special privileges.

∿

Spring was slowly approaching. The snow was starting to melt and the sun shone more frequently, but on those long spring days I was still confined to my hiding place. Nazi patrols and Belorussian police often came into the house where I was hiding, sitting down in the kitchen and demanding food and vodka from Kazimierz's wife. I was able to listen to the German visitors talking to each other and could understand what they were saying because German and Yiddish are similar. They were worried about Jewish "bandits" who had escaped from the ghettos and, together with Soviet prisoners of war, had made their way into the surrounding forests of Belorussia. Every day, they were attacking police stations and military convoys on the roads. What I heard gave me hope. These groups, called partisans, were successfully attacking my enemies.

Kazimierz soon suggested that I make contact with a partisan group he knew that was comprised of both escaped Red Army POWS and Jews from the Minsk ghetto. It was becoming extremely dangerous for Kazimierz and his family to hide me as daily patrols searched the villages and barns for Jews and Red Army fugitives. When Kazimierz talked to me about the partisans in the forest for the second time, he told me that he was in constant contact with both Jewish and Polish partisans in the forests around Slutsk, Kapyl and Koidanov.

Late one evening, I heard a knock on the door of the main house. I was terrified that a Nazi patrol had discovered my hiding place and was about to shoot me. It would have been impossible to run away since there was no window in the attic. I was horrified to think that I had escaped from a mass grave, from among the dead, and hidden all winter only to be shot in the end. I picked up the kerosene lamp, deciding that if the Nazis came into the attic, I would throw the lamp and the kerosene at them and try to run into the fields and forest.

When I heard Russian and Polish being spoken in the kitchen I realized that it was not the Nazis and their collaborators after all. Fifteen minutes later, my friend knocked on the door and said, "Michael, don't be afraid. The people in the house are our people. Open the door." In front of me stood three men with rifles on their shoulders. They were all partisans, and three others were standing on guard outside. The partisans had learned about my hiding place a short time before and told me in Russian that they would soon return to take me with them to the forest. We all said goodbye and they left the house in the dead of night.

The next morning, Kazimierz told me that the six partisans had gone to carry out a military operation and would be returning to pick me up in five or six days. Those were the longest days and nights of my young life, so badly did I want to get out of my hiding place and be free in the woods, to see daylight and the night sky again, to be with partisans who were fighting the enemy to avenge the Jewish blood that had been spilled. On the other hand, I was sad to think about leaving the family who had protected me and done all they could to keep me alive, who had loved me like their own child. They had all prayed to God for my safety and assured me that the Germans would lose the war and I would be free again. On the sixth night, the partisans arrived. When the time came to say goodbye to Kazimierz and his family, it was the first time in a while that tears had fallen from my eyes. They all cried with me.

I left with the six partisans in the middle of the night, taking a rucksack with me. We made our way through fields and forests to the area around the town of Negoreloye, where the Polish-Russian border had been located since 1939, and from there to a small hamlet called Pukhavichy, seventy kilometres southeast of Minsk. Crossing the railway tracks was not easy because the German army had guard posts every 150 to 200 metres to protect the central rail line from the partisans. This was the line that carried German military units and weapons to the front.

In the surrounding forests we came across some Jews, including some women, who had escaped from the ghettos. A few of them were carrying rifles and pistols, and they joined us en route to the base of a large group of well-armed partisans in the areas of Koidanov and Slutsk. After a few days and nights, our small group, exhausted from lack of sleep, reached the partisan camp.

We did not receive a friendly welcome, especially as Jews who had few weapons and no military training, and had brought with an eleven-year-old boy. There was no shortage of antisemitism among the partisans. The leaders were Red Army soldiers who had escaped from Nazi camps; most of them would have abandoned the Jews to their fate. We implored them to allow us to find weapons and accompany the other partisans on their military operations. Much later, even when we were able to acquire weapons by attacking Belorussian auxiliary police stations, this was still not enough for the leaders of this partisan group simply because we were Jews. In the nearby forests, where other partisan groups were located, Jews had similar experiences, but I heard of other cases where Jews were shot by partisan leaders and their deputies, sometimes just for daring to go into the villages. Inexplicably, Jews were blamed for the Nazi torture and murder of Red Army soldiers, and for the military setbacks on all the fronts. I think, also, that the Soviet partisan leaders wanted to buy the sympathy and loyalty of the local population, who were usually antisemitic. Some had already collaborated with the Germans by handing over Jewish partisans to the Nazis, as I mentioned before, in exchange for a kilogram of salt.

Sometimes, when the German army and the Belorussian police surrounded a forest where partisan groups were operating, the Soviet partisans were able to break through the blockade, but they left behind Jewish groups and their families, including children and the elderly. Without any protection or ammunition, their only chance to avoid falling into the hands of the Nazis was to try breaching the blockade by themselves.

Belorussia was under the jurisdiction of the Reichskommissariat Ostland, the Nazi occupation regime in the Baltic states headed by Hinrich Lohse, whose brutal orders were carried out quickly and efficiently. He directed decrees not only at the Jewish population, but also at Belorussians, who were deported to Germany for forced labour. He ordered the capture of Red Army soldiers and some were so mistreated that they died of starvation and typhus; others were killed after they refused to obey the orders of the German camp commandants. Many of these Red Army soldiers succeeded in escaping to join the partisans; a few who joined our group were Jewish.

In April 1942 we had twenty-two Jewish partisans in our group. Because we had all lost our own families, we felt like a family – we became brothers and sisters to one another. One of the Jews in our group, Moishe Abramowitz, who had escaped from the town of Bobruisk, had brought with him a small prayer book that he kept hidden in his boots. He helped our group cope with the difficult conditions in the forest and the tragedy of our people. Reminding us that

Passover was fast approaching, he managed to obtain some beets to make a red soup to substitute for wine, traditionally used during the holiday ritual. We had no matzah, but he dug up some horseradish from nearby fields. On the night of the first seder, we gathered near our underground bunker.

As I was the youngest, it was decided that I would ask the Four Questions, the *Ma Nishtanah*. I knew them well since, as the youngest in my family, I had always been the appropriate candidate. Here in the forest I interpreted the answers to the questions somewhat differently. In answer to the question, "Why is this night different from all other nights?" I replied, "Because last Passover all the Jews sat with their families at tables beautifully set with matzah and goblets of red wine. Last year, each of us had a goblet on our plate and listened to the oldest person in our household conduct the seder. Tonight, in the forest, our lonely and orphaned group, having miraculously survived, remembers our loved ones who were taken from us forever." Tears fell from our eyes. After this, we continued to keep the traditions of all the Jewish holidays, which gave us the courage and the will to survive. With God's help, we would eventually live in this world as free people.

In the camp, we lived in well-camouflaged underground bunkers, with twelve to fifteen people in each one. Our group was divided into those who took part in military operations and those who gathered local food from the forest and nearby villages. Through our contacts in the villages, we were able to keep informed about what was happening on the fronts and in the countries occupied by the Nazis. At the end of May that year, we heard that Reinhard Heydrich, who controlled Czechoslovakia, had been murdered by the Czech underground. In retaliation, the Nazis killed almost everyone in the villages of Lidice and Ležáky, where they thought the assassins were from. They arrested or shot all the men, sent most of the women and children to death camps and burned the villages to the ground.

In time, I got used to the woods and the partisans in our group.

Being the youngest was not always easy. Some of the partisans were afraid that if we were attacked and I, as such a young boy, was taken prisoner, I would reveal information about the location of other partisan groups. By now, our group had accumulated a number of weapons and we could plan military actions on a larger scale. Our first assignment was to destroy a police station that was twenty-five kilometres from the town of Slutsk. The Belorussian auxiliary police and German Wehrmacht soldiers at this police station had been capturing Soviets, Gypsies and Jews. A former Red Army lieutenant from the city of Gomel, a Russian by the name of Grisha Alexandrovich, was in charge of this military operation. His wife was Jewish and his relationship with Jews was, therefore, one of affection and camaraderie. He drew up a list of eight partisans to carry out the action and wanted to take me along, but some of the partisans objected, saying that I was too young. After Grisha explained to them how I could be useful, however, they agreed. I was very excited to be part of this group and to have an opportunity to take revenge.

The operation was given the name "Advance." Being small, my task was to crawl to the police station, place the dynamite and connect the wires. I left our encampment with the group in the middle of the night. We took explosives, wires and pre-assembled gasoline bombs. Each of us also carried a rifle and a pistol.

We walked through woods and fields all night long. The operation was to take place at exactly 5:30 a.m., when everyone in the police station would still be asleep. We were divided into two groups: the first would provide protection for me if I required it and the second would take up positions across the road to prevent any of the policemen from escaping alive. I was camouflaged with foliage and carried the dynamite in my rucksack.

The operation began punctually and I crawled to the barbed wire fence, pulling a long cord along behind me. I took a wire cutter out of my rucksack, cut some of the barbed wire, then went around to the back door of the station. When I got there, I placed the dynamite in contact with the fuse and carefully made my way back, crawling on my stomach and pulling the cord that was connected to the dynamite through the fence to the narrow path where my group was waiting. After we lit the end of the cord, there was an explosion a minute or so later. We lay on the ground to protect ourselves from the flying pieces of wood and brick, and then saw four half-naked policemen run from the station; they were swiftly shot by the second group of partisans. Then we all retreated, running back through the fields to the forest, where we waited for nightfall. We heard sirens and trucks speeding to the blown-up police station. Later that night we went back through the woods to our base, arriving around 3:00 a.m. We hadn't lost a single one of the partisans in our group.

The next morning, the chief commander congratulated us on our good work. Through our intelligence network we learned that fourteen Belorussian policemen in the building had been killed, all of them blown to bits, and that five policemen had been seriously injured. For our group of partisans, especially the Jewish ones, this was quite a victory. We earned a great deal of respect from the non-Jews as fighters who could strike a serious blow to our enemies. My participation in that first military operation was also a personal victory in avenging the death of my family and my people. From then until the summer of 1944, I took part in many other operations.

Partisan Operations

In the summer of 1942, the situation for Jews in the small ghettos of occupied Belorussia worsened – the Nazis were deporting people from the surrounding villages to death camps. The local Belorussian police, under the command of the Lithuanian, Latvian and Ukrainian Einsatzgruppen units, worked with the Nazis to systematically execute daily *Aktionen* and liquidate the ghettos.

I learned about the situation in Nieśwież from survivors who had escaped an *Aktion* there and joined us in the forest. They told me that the Jews in the ghetto had heard about what was happening in the nearby towns and had struck a committee comprised of youth who had belonged to various Zionist organizations or the Bund before the war. The committee had decided that if the Nazis began liquidating the ghetto, they would resist. Two Jewish girls in the group, Leah Duckar and Rachel Kagan, worked at the German weapons arsenal cleaning the rooms. The Germans trusted these girls, but as members of the underground resistance, they started to smuggle out parts of grenades, pistols and other light weapons, bringing them into the ghetto hidden under their clothes. The other young leaders of the fighting group were Shalom Cholawsky, Moshe Damesek, Berl Alperowitz, Yehoshua Mazin, Siomka Farfel, Freidl Lachovitzka and Yerahmiel Shklar. The fighting group was composed of about fifty people who worked together on deciding how to stage an armed resistance against the Nazis. They knew the consequences and vowed not to allow themselves to be taken prisoner, not to surrender themselves alive.

In mid-July 1942, members of the resistance met with Magalif, the chairman of the Judenrat, and explained that they knew that more and more Jews in the neighbouring villages were being murdered every day. The chairman guaranteed that nothing would happen to them because the Germans needed them as servants. He also warned them not to run away, telling them that those left behind in the ghetto would be held responsible. But they soon heard that a selection was planned, and on July 21, 1942, when the Nazis arrived with a new list of a few dozen workers, the resistance sprang into action. A group of young people took up positions inside the Kalte synagogue, about forty-five metres from the ghetto gate, and aimed their weapons at anyone coming through. Fighters on the synagogue roof began shooting and throwing grenades. A second group of young fighters had positioned themselves in different parts of the ghetto and when they heard the gunshots – the sign of resistance – they set fire to the houses so that the ghetto went up in flames. Whoever had the opportunity to escape ran to the surrounding fields and forests to the partisan groups.

The Germans and their collaborators fired back but they suffered losses – some were killed, others badly wounded. Having suspected that an uprising was planned, they had brought Belorussian and Lithuanian reinforcements to the ghetto gate, but by that time the entire ghetto was in flames. Approximately twenty fighters succeeded in escaping from the burning ghetto into the woods. The slogan of the Jewish resistance was "tamut nafshi im plishtim" – "Let me die with the Philistines."

The ghetto existed for eleven months, from September 1941 to July 1942. A report from the Bund that was secretly sent to London told of the uprising in Nieśwież and I heard that Jews in the Warsaw ghetto learned about it as well. This first heroic uprising is documented in an exhibit at Yad Vashem, the Holocaust memorial in Jerusalem.

~

By mid-summer, our partisan group had increased to 150 people. Throughout the year, and during the fall in our area, the Central Committee of the Communist Party in Moscow established links with several partisan groups. Under the direction of their Belorussian Headquarters of the Partisan Movement, they helped us partisans coordinate our efforts against the German occupation. Political commissars from the Soviet government helped to expand the operations against Germany.

Our enemies were definitely feeling the impact of the partisan resistance. In response, the Wehrmacht launched offensives against us, surrounding the forests and shooting at us with heavy artillery. At night, they threw rockets that lit up the woods, enabling them to drop their bombs with accuracy. In the fall of 1942 our group decided to break through the German blockade that encircled the forest where we were living and go deeper into the Bobruisk forest near the Berezina River to the base of a partisan detachment, an otriad, under the leadership of Commander Leventzow. The commissar was Comrade Lepeshkin and the group's unit took orders from Semyon Ganzenko, the head of a brigade in Western Belorussia. Our group, and our smaller detachments, joined this larger group and obeyed the orders of the Central Command. Their otriad included civilians and Red Army soldiers who had escaped from the labour camps, Jews from Bobruisk and Slutsk, and thousands of Jews who had escaped from the Minsk ghetto and brought with them a great deal of ammunition. The Minsk Jews could protect themselves and therefore didn't have to deal with the antisemitism that other Jews who had escaped into the forest did. In general, antisemitism wasn't as prevalent in the Leventzow otriad because the Bobruisk Jews had been members of the underground in the ghetto, and they were able to contribute significantly to the partisans in terms of both weapons and manpower; some had also acquired important skills from doing forced labour in the German military aerodrome.

At the beginning of 1943, parachutists from Moscow landed in our forest – they were members of the Komsomol, the youth division of the Communist Party of the Soviet Union, who had volunteered to fight with the partisans. The Central Command had recently ordered partisan groups to include Soviet citizens in the partisan fight, which automatically applied to Jews as well as non-Jews. As a result, Jewish men, women, children and the elderly were now more protected, and some partisans even provided weapons to unarmed Jews in the forest. In the early spring of 1943, Semyon Ganzenko established a partisan unit in Western Belorussia to specifically recognize and protect Jewish partisans, including women, children and the elderly. Sholom Zorin led this otriad of about four hundred partisans, most of whom were Jews from Minsk. I also heard about a detachment of around one thousand Jewish men, women and children under the leadership of Tuvia Bielski and his brothers, who had assumed responsibility for protecting and providing for all Jews, even the elderly and those who were malnourished and in poor health. To provide for all the survivors, the Jewish leaders of this partisan group set up their own self-sustaining camp, complete with workshops and a kitchen. They would come out of the forests at night and order peasants in the nearby villages to give them food and warm clothing. News of these partisan groups encouraged me to continue to fight.

I was also thrilled to learn that about two hundred Jews had escaped from the ghetto in Mir and that among them was my cousin Meir Zaturensky, who was a year older than me. Sadly, I never met up with him – I heard he was killed during an operation.

I also heard the story of a young man from my town, Shlomo Lansky, who had become an active partisan in an otriad outside Pinsk. He had been the leader of the Betar youth movement before the war and had succeeded in escaping into the forest from the Nieśwież ghetto uprising in July 1942. During one of his partisan operations he was captured, tied to a horse, dragged to a village and tortured, but he didn't reveal any information. Belorussian informants who witnessed his execution told us that when he was hanged in the public square in the town of Hancevicz, he cried out from the gallows, "I am not the first Jew and I am not the last Jew to be hanged, but we will survive you, and all you murderers will be brought to justice. We Jews and the groups of fighters in the forest will kill you wherever you are. We will give you no peace. Your bodies will be swallowed up by the swamps of Polesia."

We knew that every action we undertook was risky, and we suffered heavy casualties, but our otriad was active every day. Like the rest of the partisans – perhaps even more so – the Jews in our group continued to hope that we would outlive our enemies, that we would eventually leave the forests that had given us protection and security and return to our homes. Although many of us already knew that no one was waiting for us, that none of our family members had survived, we wanted to annihilate the collaborators who had helped murder our loved ones.

We received orders from Moscow to intensify the struggle against the Nazis, to attack them on the main roads, to tear up railway tracks that carried soldiers and heavy artillery and tanks to the front, to set fire to the bases where gasoline and oil were stored, and to destroy the police guard posts and those who manned them. Our orders were to give them no rest, day or night.

Since we now had radio contact with Moscow, we heard everything that was happening on the frontlines. We got the good news about the defeat of German Field Marshal Rommel's army in North Africa at the end of October 1942. In the Second Battle of El Alamein, the German army had lost their best tanks and weaponry and approximately 30,000 soldiers, while others had been taken prisoner. We also revelled in the news about the battle of Stalingrad: German Field Marshal Paulus and the powerful Sixth Army had surrendered on February 2, 1943. Soviet Marshal Rokossovsky, the commander of the Stalingrad front, gave them generous terms of surrender: they would not be killed. Field Marshal Paulus and twenty-two high-ranking generals were taken prisoner along with 90,000 Wehrmacht soldiers. Hitler proclaimed three days of mourning throughout Germany and all the lands occupied by the German army. We rejoiced at the news of these defeats, which indicated that Germany would lose the war.

We also heard quite a bit about Wilhelm Kube, the General-Kommissar for Weissruthenien (Belorussia) who worked out of Minsk. He was the one responsible for allowing the Jews in the Minsk ghetto to stay alive for the time being. Most were tradesmen who were forced to do a great deal of work for the German war machine – in particular to supply the Wehrmacht with underwear, uniforms, warm boots, warm coats and other items. The Jews in the Minsk ghetto knew that of all the ghettos of eastern Belorussia, theirs was the only one left, and that the same fate that befell Jews in other cities awaited them. They were well organized and kept in contact with the partisans. Often, groups of hundreds of Jews armed with weapons managed to smuggle themselves out of the ghetto and join the partisans. The Minsk ghetto ended up being liquidated in October 1943; by that time thousands of Jews, especially young people, had managed to escape into the forests.

In the fall of 1943, the Partisan Movement Staff of the Belorussian Command ordered Wilhelm Kube's assassination. A Belorussian girl by the name of Yelena Mazanik worked as a maid in Kube's residence, and lived on the premises. After many secret meetings, the partisans convinced her to carry out the attack on Commissar Kube, promising her that she would go down in history as a hero of the Soviet Union. On September 22, 1943, she placed a time-bomb under the mattress in Kube's bed. When she got off work that evening, she managed to leave the premises, despite the fact that the building was guarded by the Wehrmacht and the SS. Later, when Commissar Kube went to sleep, the bomb exploded, blowing him to pieces. The partisans were able to get Yelena safely into the woods and she worked with them until after liberation. Hitler declared a week of mourning for Kube's death and in retaliation ordered the authorities in Belorussia to kill one thousand citizens of Minsk.

Early in 1944, we received news that the siege of Leningrad had been broken; the historic city had lost hundreds of thousands of its civilians, but had not surrendered. With the daily news that the German armies were experiencing substantial losses and being forced to retreat, we expected the Allied armies to open up the second front any day, which would hasten the destruction of the Hitler regime. As the Yiddish saying goes, *az men lebt, derlebt men alles* – if you live long enough, you experience everything. Finally, the exciting news arrived from Moscow that on June 6, 1944, the Allied troops – American, British and Canadian soldiers – under the command of American General Dwight D. Eisenhower and British General Bernard Montgomery, had stormed the coast of Normandy and destroyed the German positions there. In Belorussia, the German army began retreating toward our area. All the partisan groups were ordered to be careful of retreating German soldiers, who, with the Red Army in pursuit, were trying to hide in the forests.

Eventually, the Germans surrendered to the partisan units. Defenceless and demoralized, hungry and thirsty, their uniforms dirty and in tatters, the Wehrmacht soldiers and officers begged us to spare their lives. Our orders, however, were to interrogate them and shoot them. The partisan intelligence officers extracted very important information and, although the soldiers told us that they were only following orders, among the captured were members of the SS and Einsatzgruppen officers responsible for murdering the Jewish population in the occupied areas and sending people to labour camps in Germany.

The members of the Red Army to reach our part of the forest that June were the reconnaissance groups. When we saw the columns of tanks and artillery, we celebrated, embracing and kissing the Red Army soldiers. Several Jewish soldiers and officers among them, with tears in their eyes, spoke to us in Yiddish and reassured us all that they had routed the Germans on all fronts and had taken revenge on them.

We had been liberated! Finally, we were free. We were excited, of course, but each one of us wondered where we would go once we left the forest. Most of our homes and families no longer existed. We had survived, but what awaited us?

The Red Army soldiers started clearing out the mines that the Germans had placed on roads and bridges. After they left the area, the Red Army advanced further to liberate Minsk, so we couldn't yet leave our encampment because the front was not far away. We waited impatiently for the liberation of Minsk, the capital city of Belorussia. After fierce fighting, Minsk was liberated on July 3, 1944. We prepared to leave the forest and walk to Minsk, where a grand parade was being organized for July 16. During the two-day journey to get there, as we walked through fields and along the roads, we saw destroyed German tanks and army trucks, as well as the bodies of German soldiers. From all directions, partisans walked toward Minsk with smiles on their faces, carrying their weapons and singing patriotic songs.

When we arrived in the capital, we saw a city in ruins, with most of the walls and buildings reduced to rubble. At the city centre, we stood in military columns, ready to march past the platform where the high command of the Belorussian partisans stood. Red flags and pictures of Lenin and Stalin decorated the platform. Crowds of people applauded each group and its leaders. When I marched by the high command with my unit, I heard tremendous applause for our group. The leaders made speeches in which they presented statistics on the number of military operations that had been carried out during the German occupation and the number of German soldiers and collaborators who had been killed. According to the chief commissar, 1.5 million partisans had fought in the forests against the Nazis in the German-occupied areas. Giving us all certificates stating that we had been members of the partisans, he called upon the younger partisans to enlist in the Red Army to help expedite the defeat of Nazi Germany. The rest he told to return to their former homes so they could participate in the reconstruction of their towns and cities and rebuild the local economies. At the end of the ceremony, as the orchestra played the "Internationale," everyone sang along.

The most difficult moment for me was saying goodbye – probably forever – to everyone I had lived with, as a family, over the two years in the forest. We had no addresses to give one another because none of us knew where we would end up. But we all cried tears of joy at having survived the Nazis and regained our freedom. We comforted each other with the hope that we would see each other in the future.

I left Minsk and set out in the direction of my hometown, which had also been liberated on July 3, 1944. The distance was one hundred kilometres, and I was exhausted. I had walked all the way through the forest and from there to Minsk, and I hadn't been able to sleep in the capital. It was impossible, lying on the street covered only with a military blanket. I began thinking about what awaited me in Nieśwież. It was now a town of mass graves and a hostile population that had taken every opportunity to rob Jewish homes. Many had even participated in the Einsatzgruppen killings.

As I stood beside the road on the outskirts of Minsk, Red Army soldiers drove by in trucks full of equipment on their way to the front. I was wearing a uniform that was a little too large for me and I had a rifle on my shoulder and a revolver at my side. A truck soon stopped and a Red Army soldier asked me where I wanted to go. When I answered that I was going to Nieśwież, he said he was driving in the direction of Mir. Without thinking for very long, I told him that I wanted to go with them. I knew I could figure out how to get to Nieśwież from there. I felt very comfortable among the Soviet soldiers and they let me out of the truck at the entrance to the grounds of the Prince Mirsky castle, where the Red Army was stationed with equipment and provisions destined for the front.

I hoped to find Jews who had survived in Mir, specifically my mother's brother, Gabriel Zaturensky, who had lived there. His house was in the Podol, a neighbourhood near the prince's palace and park. Before the war, I spent many summers with my cousins in my aunt and uncle's home. After half an hour of searching, I finally recognized the house. Not knowing what I would find there, my heart started pounding. I knocked on the door and an elderly Belorussian woman emerged. I told her who I was and although she was terrified at the sight of my rifle, she invited me in. I refused her offer of a glass of tea and asked her if she knew what had happened to my aunt and uncle and their family. She told me that they had all been killed in 1942 when the Mir ghetto was liquidated. Since the house was empty, the German authorities had given her permission to move in. I asked her whether there were any Jews left in the town and she said that there were a few, including the pharmacist's daughter. I later found out that my mother's other two sisters, Chana and another whose name I don't remember, also perished in the Holocaust.

I left the house and went to the centre of the town where, before the war, the world-famous Mir yeshiva had stood. As I approached the building, I saw that the window panes had been knocked out and the doors broken. Inside were workshops where the Germans had run a woodworking plant. I left the building with tears running down my cheeks as I remembered the town as it was before, with Jewish institutions and businesses. Now, hundreds of years of Jewish life had been completely erased. I headed to the road that went in the direction of the railway town of Gorodeya and shortly after, was able to stop an army truck that was going there.

When I got to Gorodeya, I asked the locals if there were any Jewish survivors, but I found no one. Before the war, one of my mother's cousins, Luba Lubetzka, had lived there with her family. Tragically, they had all been killed, along with almost the entire Jewish population, executed in the same way as the Jews in the neighbouring towns.

I then went to the road leading out of town to wait for a lift from Gorodeya to Nieśwież, now only fourteen kilometres away. Again, less than twenty minutes later, I was able to stop a Red Army truck. I asked the soldiers if they were driving in my direction and they suggested that I ride with them to a spot that was about five kilometres from my town. From there, I could walk the rest of the way. This was to be the last time that I returned to my birthplace, to the town where

I was raised, a town pulsating with Jewish life where I had played with my friends, where I had a family of aunts and uncles and cousins. I knew that all that now belonged to the past.

As soon as I got out of the truck and began to walk, my legs suddenly felt weak and my face broke into a sweat. My heart was pounding and I had trouble breathing. I thought I had a fever. The closer I got to my former home, the more I started to hate everything that I knew remained there, including all the people, many of whom bore responsibility for the murder of the Nieśwież Jews.

I will never forgive the Nazis and their barbaric collaborators. No matter how much you may learn and how many films you may see and how much you may hear, you cannot imagine what happened on that day at the mass graves.

Home No Longer

When at last I reached my hometown, I saw an elderly man in the distance coming toward me. I stopped him and asked whether he knew of any Jews who had survived and were living in town. He answered that he knew of only one, the captain of the fire brigade that was under the supervision of the military authorities. I started walking toward the fire brigade building, at the entrance to the Kazimir district. When the townspeople saw me – a young Jewish boy in a Red Army uniform armed with an automatic rifle and a revolver – they were afraid and immediately stepped off the sidewalk to walk on the street with the horses and wagons. I was reminded that under the Nazi occupation the same thing had happened to the Jews – we were not allowed to walk on the sidewalk and had to salute any Wehrmacht soldier or officer who went by. Now, when an elderly gentile woman saw me, she crossed herself, not believing that any Jews were still alive.

As I got closer to the fire brigade I began to wonder whether I could ever adjust to normal life. I had been robbed of my youth as well as my family, my friends, my town and its Jewish population. I had survived through inhuman conditions. I knew that it would take me a long time to leave behind everything that I had experienced as a young boy.

When I arrived at the fire brigade headquarters, I saw before my eyes none other than Boruch Shapiro – I recognized him right away because his younger son had been a friend of mine. We embraced and held each other tightly, tears of joy streaming down our faces. Shapiro had been one of the first Red Army soldiers to liberate Nieśwież and help organize a civilian administration. I immediately asked him whether there were any other survivors and he gave me the names of twelve in total, all of them fighters in the Nieśwież ghetto uprising who had fought in the Belorussian forests as partisans. He took me to the two houses where they were living; imagine their excitement at the arrival of a young Jewish boy – at only thirteen, I was younger than any of them. Having seen that the townspeople had taken over our homes and stolen our possessions, their morale was very low.

We survivors helped to restore order by taking over quite a few jobs in the town's provisional administration. One of the commissars gave us complete authority to track down collaborators among the local population and hand them over to the military authorities, who sent a number of them to Siberia. The non-Jewish population soon grew terrified that "their" homes would be confiscated and that they too would be sent to Siberia for collaborating with the Germans. Later on, between 1945 and 1946, others were sentenced under the military tribunals.

We began to hunt for Lithuanian, Latvian and Ukrainian collaborators, primarily looking for the leaders who had organized the eradication of Jews in Nieśwież and the surrounding areas of Baranovichi and Stolbtsy in addition to killing Red Army soldiers, partisans and Roma. I knew of a few in particular – Alexander Veronik, Alexander Leusch and Sergei Bobko. They had tried to flee with the retreating German army but were captured much later in Poland and sentenced to death by hanging.

We decided to visit the three huge pits on the grounds of the Radziwiłł Park, the mass graves where the Jews of Nieśwież had been murdered. One of them was the pit I had been in. I stood beside it for an hour without uttering a word, reliving what had happened to me on October 30, 1941. It was extremely difficult. I could not believe that

I had gotten out of that pit alive. The mass graves were neglected, covered in tall grass. A single tall old tree stood like a guardian of all the secrets about what had taken place there. The next day, we returned to cut the grass and clean up the grave site.

Two days later, we went to see the mass graves on Snów road on the outskirts of town. Before the war, people had gone there to fetch sand. Now it was where the majority of the Jews had been murdered. During the occupation, the gentile townspeople had continued to bring their wagons for sand, giving the victims no peace. We found decomposing clothing and shoes, and the bones of the dead sticking out of the sand. How strong a Jewish survivor had to be to witness all this. We suffered, anguished, and were furious with everyone who was responsible.

One of the survivors, Itshe Mazin, an artist by profession, made a wooden memorial plaque for Radziwiłł Park and inscribed – in Russian and Yiddish – words to the effect that in these graves were buried the Jews of Nieśwież who had been brutally murdered by the Nazi Einsatzgruppen and their local collaborators. Two days later, all thirteen of us were summoned to the NKVD. The officer in charge gave us twenty-four hours to remove the plaque. We didn't want to but an order is an order and we had to obey. A month later, a new plaque, inscribed solely in Russian and stating that those buried there were Soviet citizens of Nieśwież murdered by the Nazis, was placed on the graves. We had to swallow the bitter pill that the Soviet authorities were denying the martyrdom of the Jewish population of Nieśwież.

A few days after our visit to the mass graves we went to see what had happened to the oldest Jewish cemetery. It was tragic to see that most of the gravestones lay shattered and that people had removed some of them to build the foundations or front steps of their houses. The Soviet authorities at least allowed us to plant flowers on the graves.

I tried to adjust to daily life. I was given a passport that gave me the right to travel from town to town and, as a partisan, I also received a special government allotment for clothes and food as well as a monthly stipend in rubles.

In the fall of 1944, I began looking for information about my father. I wrote a letter to the military authorities in Moscow asking whether he had died or was somewhere in Russia in a military hospital. In response to my queries, I was informed that he was alive but had been injured, and was in a hospital in Tashkent in the Uzbek Soviet Socialist Republic.

The Soviet authorities gave me permission to travel to Tashkent with a special letter to present to the First Secretary of the Communist Party, Usman Yusupov, and his assistant, Comrade Muminov. I managed to get a lift to Minsk with some Soviet army soldiers but there were no passenger trains from Minsk to Tashkent; instead, I undertook a long and arduous five-day journey on various military vehicles. When I arrived at the Communist Party headquarters, I showed an official the letter addressed to Usman Yusupov and was taken to see him. He was very friendly and promised me whatever assistance I required. I was given a place to sleep and ate in their cafeteria. The next morning, a member of the militia drove me to the two military hospitals, but my father was not on either registration list. I returned, disappointed, to the secretariat, who advised me to go by train to Samarkand, where there was another military hospital. They gave me papers explaining who I was, with instructions to give me any assistance I should require.

Upon my arrival in Samarkand, I showed my papers to the chief official at the military hospital and stated the purpose of my visit. He searched through all the lists from 1942 until the present, but, again, my father's name was not listed. I became very dejected; my hopes dashed. It was a Friday and I decided to see something of the historic city, so I asked a guide whether there were any Jews in Samarkand. He told me that there were Bukharian Jews living in the city and gave me the address of their synagogue. I found my way there and met the old sexton, who invited me to come to the synagogue for services the next morning.

When I arrived on Saturday morning, I was told to take off my boots and wash my feet at the water tap. I entered the synagogue and was given a skull cap, which in Russian is called a *tyubeteyka*. It looked just like the embroidered hats that all the Uzbeks wore. Everyone was seated on the floor on oriental carpets. I was introduced to the rabbi, whom they called the *chacham*. He greeted me in Russian and invited me to eat with them in the synagogue courtyard after the prayers. During the service, the prayers and melodies were exactly like those of the Sephardic Jews of North Africa. The prayer books, printed in Livorno, were in Hebrew and Italian. All the Bukharian Jews were very friendly to me and explained how their forefathers had come there on the silk route and how they had maintained their Jewish traditions for all these centuries. After the service, we ate a meal called *plov*, which consisted of rice with lamb.

The next morning, I took the train to Tashkent. From Tashkent, it took me seven days to return to Nieśwież. It was only after the war that I received a letter from Moscow informing me that my father had fallen in the battle of Smolensk near Moscow in 1941. He had received two medals for defending the city against the German army. From then on, I accepted the fact that I was a full orphan.

~

My next plan was to go to Moscow to see my mother's cousin Israel Tzukerberg. Before the war, he had been a professor in the Dzerzhinsky Academy in Moscow and during the war he had been a colonel in the Red Army, serving on the first Belorussian front under the command of Marshal Zhukov.

At the beginning of 1945, I got a lift with the army to Minsk and then took the train to Moscow. My cousin lived in a small apartment two blocks from the Moscow State Circus of the Order of Lenin. When I arrived there I met his wife, Paulina Moiseyevna, who worked as a pediatrician in a youth institution. Paulina made an appointment for me to see Solomon Mikhoels, the head of the Jewish Anti-Fascist Committee and director of the Moscow State Yiddish Theatre from which well-known Jewish actress Dora Wasserman had graduated. I also met the great Yiddish writer Itzik Feffer and beloved Jewish actor Benjamin Zuskin. Solomon Mikhoels was very courteous and they all wanted me to stay in Moscow and enrol in the Yiddish theatre school. I decided not to, however, explaining that my dream was to go to Palestine.

Mikhoels arranged for me to meet the famous writer and journalist Ilya Ehrenburg. The meeting lasted over two hours, with Ehrenburg making notes on everything I told him about myself and the partisan movement in the Belorussian forests. He specifically wanted information about the Jewish partisans. He was planning to write a book about Jewish fighters in the Red Army and Jewish partisans because Communist leaders, including Stalin, were denying the heroic contributions made by Jewish fighters in defeating the German armies. Ehrenburg did write the book but the manuscript had to be smuggled out of the Soviet Union to the free world in 1946; parts of it, called the *Black Book*, were published in the United States and Romania that same year. In the book, Ehrenburg described the martyrdom of the Jewish people and their heroism in the struggle against the Nazis, while simultaneously revealing Stalin's hatred of the Jewish people.

After spending two weeks in Moscow, I returned to Nieśwież. The Soviet authorities had begun arresting innocent citizens, such as the honourable man I mentioned earlier, Mr. Zubowicz, who, at the beginning of the war, had risked his life and that of his children to hide, and therefore save, three Jews from Nieśwież. The Soviets had arrested Zubowicz for collaborating with the Nazis, which of course was totally fabricated. The NKVD tried to force him to sign a confession of his guilt, but he proudly refused. All of us survivors – most importantly, Jacob Lifshitz, whom he had hidden – went to Minsk to meet with the chief prosecutor and explain that Zubowicz was innocent. After spending two months in jail, Zubowicz was released. Then David Farfel and Itshe Mazin, two other Nieśwież survivors who now worked with the local NKVD, were arrested for trying to voluntarily resign from their positions. After much pressure, they too were released.

In 1945, the only good news for us was that Poland had been liberated from Nazi occupation and the Nazis were now being forced to fight on their own territory. Finally, in May 1945, Berlin fell. General Weidling, who was responsible for the defence of Berlin, ordered all the German generals and their armies to surrender. The war officially ended on May 9, 1945, and the Third Reich became history.

I soon began making plans to leave Nieśwież. Except for the graves of my family and my few survivor friends, I no longer felt any attachment to the town of my birth. As long as I live, I will remember the murderers who extinguished forever more than four hundred years of Jewish life in my hometown. I kept in mind the promise I had made to my mother that, if I survived, I would bear witness to what had happened to us. The free world had to know about the tragic destruction of six million Jews – men, women and children. It was very difficult for me to say goodbye to the survivors in Nieśwież, but they too wished to leave the town with its accursed earth and hostile population; some hoped, as I did, to reach the shores of Palestine.

In the fall of 1945, I left Nieśwież forever. After getting a lift to Baranovichi, I travelled by train to Brest-Litovsk – the birthplace of future Israeli prime minister Menachem Begin – on the Russian-Polish border, where I met some Jews who had survived the war in hiding. They warned me that the Soviet side of the border to Poland was heavily guarded and that whoever was caught trying to cross would be shot on the spot. After two days in Brest-Litovsk, I devised a plan. I took a small backpack containing my war documents and five hundred Russian rubles and went to the train station where trains carrying coal left for Warsaw every day. I had noticed that some of the coal cars were not completely closed, so I found a piece of iron pipe, jumped into one of the cars and buried myself in the coal, putting the iron pipe in my mouth so I could breathe. Thank God, I managed to get across the border; I was lucky that I didn't suffocate.

As the train slowly approached Warsaw but was still some distance from the station, I crawled out of the coal car onto the ground. While I was walking between the rails, completely covered in black soot, two Polish military policemen noticed me and asked where I had come from. They ordered me into their vehicle and drove me to a place called the Central Committee for Jews.

A secretary at the Central Committee registered me and gave me clean clothes and some soap and a towel to wash off the dirt and coal dust. When I had cleaned myself up, I sat down at a table with other Jewish survivors to eat a lunch consisting of canned meat and a bowl of bean soup. Suddenly, a young Jewish man in a Polish officer's uniform came over to our table and asked which one of us was Michael Kutz. I identified myself and he left the room, returning fifteen minutes later to ask me to follow him. In another room, he told me to pick up the telephone because someone from Lodz wanted to talk to me. Over the phone I heard the voice of a man speaking in Yiddish, asking whether I was Michael Kutz. When I said yes, he asked me what my father's name was. When I told him that my father's name was Joseph, he asked for the names of my grandparents. I answered that my grandfather's name was Tsalia and my grandmother's Chana. His voice shaking, he told me his name was Shaya, or Alexander, Kutz and that he was my father's first cousin from Rovno in Volhynia. Someone in my family was alive! I was overjoyed.

A Polish military vehicle soon pulled up in front of the centre and drove me to my father's cousin in Lodz, just over a hundred kilometres away. When we arrived at the house on Piotrkowska Street where my cousin lived with his wife, Mania, and her sister Basya, a Polish soldier armed with a rifle at the entrance to the house gave me permission to enter. Inside, I was greeted by Mania and Basya, along with some *landsleit*, townsmen, from Berezna, where my father was born. They were all extremely happy to meet another surviving member of our family. Later in the evening, my cousin Shaya came home and, as we sat at the table eating supper, I told them about myself and about the death of my family. Shaya recounted how he had escaped from the Rovno ghetto, fled to the forest and fought as a partisan.

My cousin also told me that he had graduated as an agronomist engineer before the war. After being liberated in 1944, he had enlisted in the First Polish Army as an officer under the leadership of Wanda Wasilewska and taken part in the liberation of both Warsaw and Lodz. In Lodz, he was assigned the position of chief of the Polish military police.

Many Holocaust survivors in Lodz had settled in the neighbourhood around the former Lodz ghetto, which, in August 1944, was one of the last ghettos in Poland to be liquidated. I stayed at my cousin's place for about a month and, through a Hashomer Hatzair Zionist youth group, met several boys and girls my age or a little older who were survivors of the Nazi camps. Most of the camp survivors, with their still-emaciated faces, looked like corpses, and some were still so weak that they were unable to stand. After meeting so many Jews who were physically and psychologically broken, I joined the youth group so that I could have the chance to leave Poland. At our meetings, I got to know representatives of Bricha, an organization that was helping Holocaust survivors immigrate illegally to British Mandate Palestine. Most of the Bricha members had been soldiers in the Jewish Brigade that fought with the British against the Germans on the Eastern Front.

I didn't believe that there was any future for the surviving Jews in Poland. Before the war, during a thousand years of Jewish life in Poland, the Yiddish language and culture had flourished, and Jews had helped to build the country for the benefit of all the Polish people. Nevertheless, part of that Polish population had helped the Nazis execute their plans to annihilate the Jews. There were, of course, exceptions – during the Warsaw ghetto uprising Jews received support from Polish comrades in the resistance, and some Polish families had hidden Jews, including many children, although some were well paid by those they hid. The Catholic Church in Poland and Pope Pius XII, however, had been silent about the destruction of the Jews of Poland.

After the war was over, hatred of Jews persisted. Antisemitic gangs, some of whom had belonged to the Armia Krajowa, the Polish Home Army, often dragged Jewish passengers off trains and killed them. Imagine enduring and surviving the Holocaust only to die shortly after at the hands of these Polish gangs. Later on, in July of 1946, with the Soviet army still present, Polish police in the town of Kielce stood by during a pogrom that resulted in the deaths of forty Jews. Only when the pogrom had subsided did the police arrive to restore order.

It was this history and still-present hatred that made me decide to leave the people and the country of Poland, a place the Nazis had chosen as the mass grave for European Jewry. In November 1945, Bricha members advised me of a plan and I, along with a group of young people, took the train two hundred kilometres to Wrocław, Silesia, which had been decimated by Soviet artillery when the German soldiers retreated. But when we arrived in Wrocław, a detachment of the Armia Krajowa, the Polish resistance movement who often attacked or killed Jews, shot at us from the ruins of the city walls. We all ran, zigzagging to dodge the flying bullets, and barely succeeded in reaching the next train station, which was a long way on foot. Once we got there, we had to wait four hours for a train to Wałbrzych, about eighty kilometres away.

We stayed in a grand house in Wałbrzych that had previously belonged to a *Volksdeutsche*, an ethnic German. Then, late one night, we travelled the approximately twenty kilometres to the border between Poland and Czechoslovakia, where we were able to bribe a Polish border guard to let all of us cross. On the other side of the border, the Czech army received us very well and drove us about sixty kilometres to the town of Náchod. We were taken to a large barracks surrounded by barbed wire and given a hot meal, warm blankets and straw mattresses. The next morning the army drove us to the train station to travel to a displaced persons (DP) camp in Bratislava, a few hundred kilometres away.

Although the war had ended and the ghettos and the Nazi camps were gone, as was the need to hide or fight as partisans, Jews were now living in DP camps that had been set up for refugees from Nazi-occupied Europe. Many didn't want to stay in the camps and were travelling from one country to another, crossing borders illegally to reach the shores of our Jewish homeland, the Land of Israel. The British authorities, however, had locked the gates of our homeland and were not allowing the Jewish survivors to enter.

During World War II, the British people had fought our common enemy and endured bombings day and night in cities such as London, Leeds, Liverpool and Manchester. Now, however, their country had enforced a strict immigration policy that caused more hardship and suffering for the remnants of the Jewish people in addition to, in my opinion, closing its eyes when Arabs attacked Jews. In the spring of 1946, the Attlee government issued a new White Paper, a document that allowed only 100,000 certificates, based on humanitarian grounds, for Jewish refugees to legally immigrate to Palestine. For us, this was not a solution – it was nothing, considering the numbers of Jews who had been left to languish in the displaced persons camps. Despite the fact that the leaders of the British government, prime minister Clement Attlee and foreign minister Ernest Bevin, had taken a pro-Arab position in British Mandate Palestine, and although the journey was long and difficult, a significant number of Jewish youth were intent on reaching the Land of Israel. As survivors, we had the courage and determination to get there.

The DP camp in Bratislava was a transit camp from which many Jewish refugees tried to make their way to Austria. The camp was extremely overcrowded, without sufficient sanitation. An organization called the American Jewish Joint Distribution Committee, or the Joint, however, did supply everyone with adequate food. There were also emissaries from Eretz Yisrael there, and fierce competition among the various Zionist organizations to attract more members, especially young people.

Along with some of the other young Jewish refugees, I joined the Betar youth organization, which was illegal in Poland and Czechoslovakia because it supported the Irgun, the underground paramilitary organization fighting against the British Mandate authorities in Palestine. As a result, many of the leaders of other Jewish organizations in the camp – who were not as militant – considered us traitors to the Jewish people. But having served in the partisans, I was attracted to Betar.

After staying in Bratislava for five weeks we made up our minds to leave the camp and try to cross into Austria. Bricha instructed us to leave all our documents, medals and personal photographs with them because the Red Army guards at the Austrian border were very strict about conducting thorough searches. Unfortunately, I never got any of these possessions back. We were also advised not to speak Yiddish, Russian, Polish or German among ourselves. We had to remain silent. The only answer we were to give the border guards was that we were Greek; one of us had also learned how to say in Greek that we had worked for the Nazis as slave labourers in fields or factories and were now returning home.

On December 25, 1945, we arrived at a bridge where a border guard searched our bags and the pockets of our trousers and coats, then asked us who we were. As instructed, we all responded, "Greek." The guard, not knowing what to do with this group of seventeen boys and girls, cursed us in Russian and, using hand gestures, ordered us to hurry up and leave the bridge because we were holding up traffic for the Red Army. We had to walk roughly sixty kilometres to the Soviet-administered zone of Vienna, one of four Allied zones in the city. The other three zones were American, British and French. From the Soviet zone, we were allowed to cross into the American zone.

Exhausted, we reached the Rothschild Hospital, another displaced persons camp under the authority of the Joint. Someone led us to a very big room where each of us was assigned to a narrow bed with a straw mattress, a pillow and a blanket. We were also given new underwear, new shoes and enough to eat. We were told that these arrangements were only temporary because more and more Jewish refugees were arriving every day and we would have to make room for them. At the camp, we met Jewish soldiers from the Jewish Brigade who helped us in any way they could. We also met representatives of Zionist parties who conducted constant propaganda campaigns against one another. The Haganah and the Irgun, especially, disagreed with each other on immigration strategies, and sometimes came to blows. But we were all united in our goal of reaching the Land of Israel. We knew that a long, challenging journey lay ahead of us.

Every day in the Rothschild Hospital, as well as in the neighbouring streets, we held demonstrations against the Mandate policies even though we had no permits to do so. We carried placards with appeals to the Special Commission of the United Nations Relief and Rehabilitation Administration (UNRRA) and the American State Department. We wanted them to hear our cries, our suffering and our pain: "Let our people go to Israel!"

The camp administrators were anxious for us to leave as soon as possible because our Betar youth group was very militant. The British authorities approached the American authorities, telling them that our group had smuggled ammunition into the hospital, and that we were using the place for training in the use of weapons. As a result, the British military police received permission from the American authorities to enter our room and forcibly remove us. At 7:00 a.m. the next day they marched in with their automatic weapons and ordered us to dress quickly, pack up our belongings and leave immediately. We argued that they didn't have the right to evict us, but they ejected us by force anyway. We tried to resist, but the soldiers outnumbered us and pushed us into their military vehicles. We sang "Hatikvah" – the anthem of many Zionist groups – at the top of our voices as we were driven to the train station, so the sound could be heard through the streets of Vienna. At the station we were put into empty train cars and the UNRRA gave us canned meat, bread and cigarettes. The doors of the cars were locked from the outside and guarded by British military patrols until the train left the station.

We travelled all night without knowing where they were taking us. When the train stopped, the American military police and representatives of UNRRA opened the doors, ordered us to stand in line and then walk to another DP camp by the name of Franz Josef Kaserne. We were in Salzburg. In the camp, which in Yiddish and Hebrew was called Camp Herzl, we were registered and given identity cards. The overcrowding and poor sanitary conditions are almost impossible to describe and the barracks, where each of us received a small army cot, a straw mattress and a green blanket, were unheated. Although we were given soap every day, there was not enough hot water. As for meals, we stood in long lines to receive our allotted portions. People who had a little money could go into town and purchase some food, but those who had nothing went hungry and often stole from one another. Here also, soldiers from the Jewish Brigade helped us a great deal, giving us chocolate and oranges, as well as army boots, blankets, cigarettes and uniforms. There were quite a few tailors in the camp who fixed my trousers and jackets in exchange for food.

When the Austrian population of Salzburg saw us in the British uniforms we had gotten from the Jewish Brigade, they avoided us, but the way we were dressed did not bother the American military police. My friends and I often left the camp to tour the city, which was very beautiful, with clean streets, tree-lined boulevards and statues. I particularly enjoyed the architecture of the great cathedral where Mozart played. Salzburg had been luckier than other cities in that it had not been heavily damaged during the war.

Camp Herzl was extremely overcrowded, with Jews arriving each day from places like Vienna. To make room for the newcomers and reduce the overcrowding, the administration once again ordered our group to leave the camp. We packed our rucksacks and were driven in army vehicles to catch the train to the spa town of Bad Gastein. As I stepped off the train, I was enchanted by the view of the mountains and the natural beauty all around the town. Before the war, Bad Gastein had been world-famous for its waterfalls and hot mineral springs that flowed from the Alps. The town had a lot of hotels and guesthouses, as well as a beautiful auditorium located in the high Gamskogel Mountains.

Our group settled comfortably in the Hotel Struber. Boys and girls were assigned to separate rooms, unlike the camps where men and women of all ages, including children, had slept in the same room. In accordance with a UNRRA directive, the Jewish refugees pretty much occupied all the hotels while the hotel owners were permitted to live in only a single room. The Austrians in Bad Gastein were not pleased that the survivors had taken over all the hotels – they regarded us as ill-mannered and culturally inferior foreigners. In turn, the Holocaust survivors viewed the Austrians as German collaborators who had assisted in the destruction of European Jewry. We often reminded them that Adolf Hitler was a son of their great cultured nation. We also reminded them that in 1938, right after the *Anschluss* – the annexation of Austria into Nazi Germany – they had perpetrated pogroms against Jewish people, confiscating their homes and businesses, deporting them to concentration camps and physically destroying hundreds of years of Jewish life in a country where the Jews had made significant contributions in the fields of science, medicine, banking and commerce. Now, when Austrians emerged, drunk, from their beer gardens and caught sight of us on the narrow streets, they shouted, "Verfluchte Juden! [You damned Jews!] It's a shame that the Führer did not finish his work." We would beat them up, but run and hide when the American military police arrived to arrest us. The Austrians were waiting impatiently for Bad Gastein to be *judenrein* again.

The UNRRA played a big part in our daily lives, as did the Joint Distribution Committee. The UNRRA opened a warehouse beside the train station from which they supplied all the hotels with food and the Joint provided us with clothing. A group of Zionists in Bad Gastein elected a community council that maintained order together with a Jewish police force. They all wore uniforms provided by the American military authorities.

I was chosen from among the young people to join the police. Every morning at 6:30 a.m., we took the chairlift to the top of the Gamskogel. Our group's instructor, Moishe, was originally from Rovno and had been in the Red Army during the war. For two hours a day, he taught us how to use weapons and explosives such as hand grenades. Like several others who had served as partisans or in the army, I already knew how to handle ammunition and could also teach the other young people.

There was a small chalet on the mountain peak that the Austrians used to get to by donkey, bringing food and bottles of beer with them. We regularly climbed to the peak and I became skilled in alpine mountain climbing. When we reached the top of the mountain, we raised a blue and white flag and sang "Hatikvah." My thoughts wandered back to the historic rebellion against the Romans two thousand years ago at the ancient hilltop fortification of Masada in Judea. Upon returning from the summit, I resumed my police work, which consisted of maintaining order and helping to distribute packages from the UNRRA to Jewish refugees.

There was a hospital a few kilometres away in the small resort town of Bad Hofgastein, and whenever someone from the camp required medical attention, the Jewish police drove them there by ambulance. The hospital had two doctors, one a surgeon and the other, strangely enough, a former SS officer who was there because his skills were badly needed. The Americans guarded him closely. The Jewish patients didn't want to wear the hospital pyjamas because they looked like concentration camp uniforms, so the hospital administrator gave them permission to wear their own clothing.

As time passed, the situation in the DP camps in Austria and

Germany became very tense. The American authorities often criticized the Jewish police for ignoring situations in the camps that they thought warranted investigation, such as black market activities, and the United Nations Commission sent representatives to visit the camps. We continued to organize demonstrations, marching through the streets carrying placards with slogans such as, "Let the Jews go to Palestine," and shouting into microphones, "Down with the Bevin and Attlee policies!" But nothing changed. The gates to Eretz Yisrael remained locked.

We resented the UN and the four Great Powers – the US, Britain, France and the Soviet Union. We had survived the Holocaust, lost our families, our homes and six million of our people, and still we were drifting from country to country only to end up in DP camps with inadequate conditions, where three times a day we had to line up with bowls to receive our allotted portion of food. The gentile world had not learned about, and did not want to understand, the suffering that Jews had endured, the inhuman conditions that had brought us to the lowest point in human history, in which not only had the majority of the Jewish people been killed, but among those murdered in the mass graves and crematoria were more than 1.5 million innocent children. The Nazis and their collaborators had taken everything away from us except our dignity and our will to live. We survivors would never forget our ancestral homeland, which God had given us. We would break the chains of our two-thousand-year exile and eventually reach the shores of pre-state Israel.

Our brothers and sisters in Palestine had shouldered the responsibility for fighting against the policies of the British Mandate government. The Haganah, the Irgun and the Stern gang all intensified the struggle to force the British authorities to abandon the Mandate in Palestine. The *Yishuv*, Jewish residents there, did everything possible to help bring Jewish survivors to the shores of the Mediterranean Sea, and from there to kibbutzim, collective farms, where they could blend in with the local population and avoid falling into the hands of the British police. If the British authorities caught illegal immigrants, they sent them to holding cells in Cyprus where they were put into camps behind barbed wire under military guard. Considering that many of these Jews, not long before, had been imprisoned in Nazi camps behind electrified wire fences under the strict surveillance of guards with vicious dogs, this treatment made them feel extremely fearful and anxious.

I received instructions from the Jewish Brigade to travel to a DP camp in Linz, about two hundred kilometres away, where I met members of the Irgun who had amassed a large quantity of ammunition. This valuable merchandise had to be smuggled to the underground in Palestine, which was not an easy undertaking. The British intelligence services were always on alert, watching our every move. In order to do this, I needed to ask a favour of the vice-president of the camp in Linz, Mr. Goldberg, whom I had met, along with his family, in 1939. When they fled from the Nazi occupation of Lodz, they had managed to steal across the border to Soviet-occupied Belorussia and had come to Nieśwież. In 1942, he and his family escaped from the burning Nieśwież ghetto into the forests and joined the partisans. In the summer of 1944, when Nieśwież was liberated, he and his family returned to the town and I met him again, but he, too, did not want to remain there. He went back to Poland and eventually ended up in Linz. Goldberg helped us obtain documents for members of the Jewish underground that allowed them to legally live in the DP camp and the surrounding area. He also showed us how to disassemble weapons and find a way to smuggle them into Italy.

Our plan, which was not easy, was as follows: we would move from the American zone into the British zone, from the British zone into the French zone, and from there to Italy and the Mediterranean, where we would board small fishing boats and try to break through the British blockade to the coast of Palestine. It would take considerable time and tremendous courage to avoid being intercepted by the British sea patrols. Our assignment quickly expanded to include obtaining more weapons in Salzburg, Linz and Graz. We chose Salzburg as our centre because freight trains travelled from there to Innsbruck, which was close to the Italian border.

At Camp Herzl in Salzburg, we packed the ammunition and weapons in wooden boxes and stamped the boxes to indicate that they contained cans of food being sent to the camp in Innsbruck by the UNRRA. We transported the boxes at night, in jeeps driven by men who wore UNRRA uniforms so that they wouldn't be stopped at the entrance to the freight yard. We knew ahead of time which train cars were going to Innsbruck, so we carefully removed the seals from the doors, placed our boxes inside, closed the doors and put the seals back exactly as they were. We had people standing guard around us to ensure that we hadn't been noticed, especially by the American military police. In Innsbruck, our comrades were waiting impatiently. They already knew which train cars were "ours" and when the train arrived, they very carefully unsealed the doors of the correct cars and unloaded the boxes onto a truck. There, too, the drivers wore the uniforms of the UNRRA, and they also had documents that would enable them to cross the Brenner Pass to Mirano, Bolzano and Trento, driving through Milan and Cremona to La Spezia. There, the boxes would be loaded onto boats for transport to British Mandate Palestine.

By the time we returned to Bad Gastein it was the fall of 1946. We soon received an order from Bricha to be prepared to leave once again for Salzburg, where we boarded old train cars travelling to Innsbruck. To get there, we had to go through the British-occupied zone and the guards searched all of us thoroughly. Our certificates from the UNRRA were in order but they still asked us whether we belonged to a Zionist terrorist organization and why we wanted to go to Innsbruck. We answered that we had to make place for new DPs who were still streaming into the Austrian DP camps. They let us pass through. When our train arrived in Innsbruck, which was luckily in the French-occupied zone of Austria, the French army examined our papers and they too found everything in order.

From the train station, we were taken by truck to a DP transit camp that we called Sammy's Place – I'm not sure what its official name was. Sammy was in charge of Bricha in the area of the Brenner Pass, which was the transit point to reach Italy, and a Bricha member told us how to get across it. In this camp, as well, the Zionist military groups were at odds with each other. It was difficult to cool their tempers because the head of Bricha, a leftist, was not always neutral.

On our fifth day in the camp, late at night, I boarded one of a few trucks with a group of about 150 people. After two hours of driving, we arrived at our destination near the Brenner Pass and proceeded along a narrow path covered in deep snow, which was very difficult for children and older people. The young people helped them out, giving the children chocolate to keep them from crying. It was bitterly cold, around -25 degrees Celsius. Our hands and feet froze and our faces turned red – our shoes and clothing were too light for that weather. We got through the Pass without being noticed by the French border patrol, but we had to be more careful as we approached the Italian border patrol and its Carabinieri, the military police force. When we came to a slope, we had to throw our bags down one at a time and then slide down on our behinds. The young people slid down first so they could help the children and the elderly on the other side.

On the Italian side, not far away, the Bricha people were waiting for us in army trucks, dressed in the military uniforms of the Jewish Brigade. They drove us about three hundred kilometres to a small hotel in the town of Mirano where we had the opportunity to warm up and eat a hot bowl of soup and tea biscuits. The young children were given hot chocolate and hot milk. Then we left the hotel for the train station, where we were put in unheated train cars that would take us all to a UNRRA transit camp in Milan.

Italy

From the central train station in Milan we were driven to the intake camp Scuola Cadorna, where we were registered and given documents by both the UNRRA and the Italian *questura* (police) stating that we were *stranieri* (foreigners). The transit camp was filled with Jewish refugees of all ages. Each group that arrived had to wait for two to three weeks to be transferred to the various other camps in northern Italy. Here, as in all the other places, the different Zionist organizations, led by *shlichim*, emissaries from Eretz Yisrael, competed with one another to attract members.

Many of us, to escape the crowded conditions in the camp, took long walks through the city. I didn't know a single word of Italian, but I still tried to communicate with people who seemed friendly. Locals often invited us to drink a cappuccino with them and some invited us for meals in restaurants or in their homes. My comrades and I had the opportunity to visit many parts of the city, including the building that housed La Scala, the local opera, and the grand historic cathedral, with its beautiful sculptures by Italian artists. These buildings take up a few blocks in the centre of the city. We also visited museums and art galleries, acquainting ourselves with the great art of the Italian people. When I was a child, I browsed through my parents' art magazines from Italy and other European countries, so I was eager to see the magnificent art for myself.

After four weeks in Milan, near the end of January 1947, we left for the Grugliasco DP camp, about four kilometres west of Torino. The camp was enclosed by a high iron fence and gate because it had been a psychiatric hospital during the war and the tall buildings were surrounded by trees, flowerbeds and rose gardens. The Jewish administration of the camp, along with some of the Jewish police and representatives of the UNRRA, all in military uniforms, welcomed us and told us that we had to respect the camp's boundaries. They registered us and gave us identity cards in both English and Italian.

The most pressing problem in the Grugliasco camp was finding space for us to sleep and store our small suitcases or backpacks. The rooms were packed with men, women, children and the elderly all mixed together. Families used blankets hanging on wires to enclose their space. Unfortunately, there was no wood to burn, so the room was very cold. Instead, we burnt newspaper and twigs we had collected from the trees outside, only a few at a time, so as not to be detected by the camp police. The lavatories in each building were for both men and women, and it was impossible to keep them clean. We waited in line to use them, as was the case with the showers. The UNRRA provided food but we still had to stand in long lines, give our names and show our identity cards before receiving our meal. The Joint gave us shoes and clothing that were either too big or too small, but we managed to exchange them with one another.

Some DPs had relatives in the US who sent them packages of clothing, food and US dollars, which greatly improved their situation because it meant they could go to the market square in Torino to sell or trade these items. Each one of us began searching for relatives in the US, Argentina or South Africa, anywhere so that we would be able to leave the DP camp and possibly immigrate to one of those countries. By this time I was starting to lose hope of reaching Palestine, aware that England was not about to abandon the Mandate voluntarily.

I knew that my maternal grandmother's sister, Alte Basitches, was in North America, but I didn't know exactly where she lived. I recalled that the city where she lived was either something that sounded like "Flifland" or Cleveland. I purchased a map of North America and located the town of Flin Flon, Manitoba, in Canada, and the city of Cleveland, Ohio, in the US. In the meantime, I contacted an Italian citizen of Torino whose name was Senior Dante. He was a government worker in a high position and was sympathetic to the Jewish refugees in the camps. He suggested that I write a letter to Eleanor Roosevelt who, at the time, was involved in the United Nations as an advocate for children all over the world, to ask her to help me find my relatives in North America. Having a good command of English, he wrote the letter to Mrs. Roosevelt in New York on my behalf. A month later I actually received a reply from her! The letter said that she had found my grandmother's sister and her children, and had told them about me and given them my address in the camp. Ten days later I received an envelope from my family in Cleveland containing a letter, their photographs and the sum of twenty dollars. I was thrilled to know that I had relatives in America – it made me feel much less alone in the world. My aunt and her children wanted to know what had happened to our large family and the Jews of Nieśwież; with difficulty, I described what had happened and how I had survived.

My family did what they could to bring me to Cleveland, but the US quota for refugees from Poland was very restricted and the waiting period for a visa was long. On several occasions my relatives helped me out materially, which allowed me to share what I received with friends like George Geller from Lodz, who had miraculously survived a few different Nazi camps. George worked for the small medical clinic in the DP camp, driving the ambulance back and forth between the clinic and the hospital in Torino. Through him, I got temporary work as his assistant.

To pass the time, young people in the DP camps took part in sports like soccer and volleyball. They named their teams things like Maccabee and Hapoel, and played against teams in other DP camps, especially the nearby camp in Rivoli, just four kilometres away.

There were various Zionist groups in Grugliasco, as there were in the DP camps in Austria, and the underground – both the Haganah and the Irgun – were very active as well. The latter two groups organized big demonstrations of men, women and children marching in the streets with placards proclaiming, "Down with the policies of Attlee and Bevin!" Foreign journalists photographed the demonstrations and the pictures were published in newspapers all over the world. They also wrote articles decrying the fact that after the war, Jewish Holocaust survivors had to languish in the DP camps of Europe. Various UN commissions and representatives of the US government visited our camp to see the situation for themselves.

In Italy, Bricha and the underground worked together somewhat to rent small fishing boats to bring more refugees to pre-state Israel. But a large number of these boats were stopped by the British naval blockade and their passengers were forcibly loaded onto British navy ships and taken to Cyprus. The refugees nevertheless continued to have courage and hoped that eventually they would reach the shores of our ancestral homeland.

I repeatedly implored the leader of the Bricha to allow me to go on one of the boats, but the answer was always no. He explained that I was useful to them for various reasons, one being that I had picked up the Italian language very well. "Your work here is not finished," he said. "You are young and healthy, and you have experience in the underground. You must remain here for now, until your time comes."

There was constant contact and, though rare, sometimes even cooperation between the Haganah and the Irgun in the DP camps in Italy. As part of a small group of young people in the underground, I met a man named Yehuda; no one knew his last name. He helped rent the fishing boats that took the refugees to Palestine, sending as many young people as possible on these ships in the hope that they could break through the British naval blockade.

During my stay in Italy I also had the opportunity to meet Dov Shilansky, who was the head of the Irgun in Italy in 1947. He was carefully guarded by a special elite group of young members of the underground, so it was difficult to meet with him personally. I met with him on three occasions, usually near the town of Arona. He spent a lot of time with me and shared information, speaking very slowly, carefully weighing every word.

I visited many DP camps to establish contact with members of the underground, most frequently travelling between the camps at Cremona and Rivoli. When people in my camp asked me why I travelled around so much, I told them that I had *landsleit* from the small towns of Berezna and Sarny in Cremona and the other camps, and showed them photographs of me with the *landsleit*.

The Jewish underground was very careful about the British intelligence service in Italy, whose agents kept an eye on us in all parts of the country. Somehow, we were still able to smuggle young people and ammunition into Palestine. Some Italians worked with us, for the most part without payment, because they felt a great deal of sympathy for the Jewish refugees. They also harboured resentment toward the English because of the number of civilian deaths they had caused when the Allied forces bombed Italy during the war, and they resented Britain's control over former Italian colonies.

Eventually my work expanded and I was sent to Rome – not far away was the DP camp Cinecittà, where the underground was very active. My task was to help them organize demonstrations in Rome against the British Mandatory Authority in Palestine. During one of the largest demonstrations that we organized, we marched to the Arch of Titus holding signs with the Latin inscription *Judea Capta*. It did not take us long to hang a placard with the Italian inscription *Judea Libero* and the Hebrew saying *Am Yisrael Chai*, which means the people of Israel live. The Italians and the *carabinieri* watched but did not intervene.

When I travelled to a DP camp in the town of Bari on the Adriatic Sea, I happened to meet Moshe, Yankl and Hinda Kutz, siblings who were my father's cousins from the town of Rokitno in Volhynia. I was

overjoyed that some other members of my father's family had survived. During the war, they had fought in the surrounding forests as
partisans. Moshe and Yankl were connected to the underground and
also helped to smuggle weapons into pre-state Israel.

As time passed, my family in Cleveland grew more anxious for me
to join them – I was the only survivor of our entire family in Nieśwież.
My cousins had submitted an application to US immigration for me
to get a visa but were told that there was still a two-year wait. They
were then advised to hire a lawyer by the name of Harry Zaitzik, who
suggested they apply for a student visa for me. I eventually received
a letter from the American ambassador in Rome informing me that
I would have to wait a long time for the student visa as well. It wasn't
until 1949 that I was finally able to meet my family in Cleveland, and
by that time I was able to travel there from Canada.

At the beginning of 1948, rumours were circulating in the
Grugliasco camp that the Dominion of Canada, in conjunction with
the Canadian Jewish Congress, would bring five hundred Jewish
children and youths to Canada from Italy. My name was on a list of
young people who were told to contact Dr. Adam, the northern Italy
representative of the Joint in Milan. Dr. Adam was originally from
Lemberg, now the Ukrainian city of Lviv, and his job was to collect
the young people from all the DP camps. He helped us all obtain
the necessary documentation and Displaced Persons Certificates of
Identity from the UNRRA. The Canadian consul in Rome then sent
us to doctors for medical examinations. Only then did we get permission to legally immigrate to Canada. I would soon take the train to
Genoa, where I would sail on the Greek ship *Nea Hellas* to Canada.

I began making preparations for the journey. Like a lot of my
friends, I found myself in the dreadful situation of having to sever
contact with people I had worked with and who I now considered
close friends. I went to say goodbye to all my friends and acquaintances, knowing that this would be the last time that we would see
each other. Since 1945, many of us young people had been as close

as brothers and sisters, having made the long journey to Italy together. Among the young people who left the Grugliasco DP camp with me were my friends Micky Hoch, Ben Blum, Alex Binkovich, Joseph Hoffer and his brother, Leizer, Chaim Tager, Saul Spitz, Saul Halperin, Jack Goldman, Isaac Messinger and George Geller.

We left from Genoa on March 10, 1948. On board the ship, I met more people I knew from Rome and I was also reunited with the Lorberg brothers, my friends from Cremona. By chance, I also met up with my friend David Gurevich and his girlfriend, Gitele, with whom I had made long and difficult journeys through the various DP camps in Italy. Thelma Tessler, a social worker for the Jewish Family and Children's Service in Winnipeg, Manitoba, accompanied us on our voyage and on March 21, 1948, we docked in Halifax, Nova Scotia.

Finding a New Home

Upon our arrival in Halifax, we were greeted by members of the Jewish community, along with the press and representatives of the Nova Scotia government. They all made speeches welcoming us to Canada. That evening was Purim and the Jewish community had arranged a reception for us at the Young Men's Hebrew Association, the YMHA, where we received presents from Jewish youth. For the next two days we stayed with various Jewish families – I stayed with the Morrisons, who had helped many Jewish refugees settle in Halifax. Next, we were divided into groups according to whether we were moving to Montreal, Toronto, Winnipeg or Vancouver. I was on the list to go to Winnipeg, as were some of my friends. On the third day, we left Halifax by train accompanied by Alistair Stewart, Co-operative Commonwealth Federation (CCF) Member of Parliament for Winnipeg. The CCF later became the New Democratic Party. Alistair Stewart was a kind, warm person who treated us as a father would.

When we arrived at the Winnipeg train station, we were met by a delegation from the Canadian Jewish Congress that included its chairman, Mr. Solomon; the mayor of Winnipeg, Mr. George Sharpe; and representatives from the Joint. Representatives of the Manitoba government made speeches and all the newspapers, most notably the *Winnipeg Free Press,* printed articles with our photos. The articles wished us well in our newly adopted country and maintained that, in time, we would contribute to making the province a better place for the entire population.

In the train station we waited once again to be assigned to Jewish homes. It was not long before a young social worker named Rose Parker approached me with a middle-aged Jewish couple who introduced themselves as Mr. and Mrs. Glassman. Mr. Glassman invited me to go with them and when he asked me where I was from, I recognized his Yiddish dialect as being from Volhynia. We drove to their home at 379 Scotia Street and they told me I could stay in their daughter Miriam's room until the end of June. She was away studying at Columbia University in New York and when she returned home, they would decide where to move me.

It was very hard at first for me to adjust to a normal life, to having a room of my own, a bed with clean sheets, and all the comforts of home after seven difficult years of wandering, with seldom anyplace to rest. I had always been on the move. But I was still really young, and my will to live and the memory of my mother's last words to me helped me overcome all these hardships and go on.

The Glassmans treated me as my own parents would have and the Jewish community in Winnipeg did whatever they could to help us get settled, find work and begin our new lives. We attended English classes at the YMHA on Albert Street and some of the young people in our group started to learn trades. I got a job working for Manny and Alan Nozick at the Nozick Commission Company, which was also on Albert Street. I quickly learned to take care of their stock of very exclusive ladies' clothing, which they exported all over Canada.

I also joined Winnipeg's amateur Yiddish theatre group housed in the building belonging to the Hebrew Sick Benefit Association on Selkirk Street. Under the guidance of its director, Hyman Roller, I performed in a play about early nineteenth-century Jewish humourist Hershele Ostropoler in the Playhouse Theatre on March 21, 1949. The production was very successful and the money from ticket sales went to the Zionist Farband organization of She'erit Hapletah (surviving remnants) to help new immigrants come to Winnipeg. For the most part, I think that Jewish immigrants adjusted very quickly to normal life. It helped to become members of Jewish and community organizations; we grew quite close to one another, often feeling like brothers and sisters. I worked with Jewish youth from Winnipeg on various projects for the welfare of our community and was very grateful to them for their understanding, loyalty and friendship.

Eventually, near the end of 1949, I contacted friends who had settled in Montreal and they suggested that I join them there. It was very hard for me to make the decision to leave my devoted family – the Glassmans had given me a home filled with love and comfort. They had even offered to pay for my education. Since childhood, however, I had always been independent, so I refused their offer. I was not a yeshiva student who needed to be supported and, even if I couldn't support myself, I didn't want to accept their generosity. In the end, I decided to leave Winnipeg. Saying goodbye to them and the friends who had come with me from Italy was very emotional. I told them all that I would never forget them because they had all become part of my family. I have kept my word to each and every one of them all these years. When the Glassmans drove me to the train station, they even gave me back all the rent money I had insisted on paying while I lived with them.

Over the years, the friends I left in Winnipeg formed a group called ANAV (Ezrat Noar Vaed, Help Youth Forever) to raise money to help disadvantaged children in Winnipeg and the rest of Canada. On the 25th anniversary of our coming to Canada in 1948, this group held the first reunion of war orphans, which I attended. By this time, our survivor group was spread out all over Canada, the US and South America. Many came from as far away as Venezuela, California, Vancouver, Saskatoon, Boston, Montreal and Toronto.

After that initial and very successful reunion, the group held one every five years until the 60th anniversary, which was held in the 59th year due to the aging of the group. I attended them all, and to this day, I keep in touch and maintain a bond with the few remaining survivors of our core group.

~

When I arrived in Montreal, I got in touch with the friends who had been in Italy with me. Morris Stern, who, like me, had started out in Winnipeg, was now the social director of Ostrowski's Hotel in Saint-Faustin, Quebec, and he suggested that I get a job as a waiter there. The work paid well, so I did, and I helped him entertain the guests in the evenings. The famous actress, playwright and theatre director Dora Wasserman, who recited Yiddish magnificently, was also an entertainer at the hotel. At the end of the summer I returned to Montreal, where I found a job in a furniture factory for the Colonial Chesterfield company. I learned about furniture production quickly and within a short time became a section foreman. In the evening I took English classes at the YMHA, which was near Fletcher's Field and the beautiful Mount Royal.

In the early 1950s, with several other young people, I helped found the Dov Gruner youth club under the auspices of the Betar Zionist movement in Montreal. Sam Sokoloff, the president of the Fleetwood television company, provided us with financial assistance, as did Mr. Morris Finston, the head of Finbo Dress Man. I became very active in various *landsmanshaftn* (organizations with people from my region); Histadrut, a labour organization that supported new immigrants to Israel; and other Jewish and non-Jewish organizations. I also participated in fundraising for the Combined Jewish Appeal (Federation CJA) and the Red Feather Campaign, an annual fundraising drive for more than thirty welfare agencies in Montreal.

In 1956, I joined the Order of the Knights of Pythias, an organization whose members visit community centres and hospitals, bringing entertainment and refreshments. We helped the Sun Youth organization arrange sports activities for young people from poor districts, providing them with uniforms and sports equipment. Every

Saturday, we visited children at the Montreal Children's Hospital, bringing them toys and refreshments and singing songs with them. Every December, we arranged a party for the children, most of whom were bedridden or in wheelchairs, as well as for diabetic children from Camp Kanawana. Our organization's donations helped create one of the largest science libraries at the hospital.

Through the Knights of Pythias, I also visited hundreds of war veterans from World War i and World War ii in the military hospital in Ste-Anne-de-Bellevue, providing entertainment, refreshments and cigarettes. Once a month, we visited the elderly in the Jewish Old Age Home, opposite the beautiful park on Esplanade Avenue. I was the social chairman of certain projects and organized trips for the residents through the generosity of the Maislin brothers, who donated trucks from their company so we could take the residents to see the Ice Capades and the Ice Follies at the Montreal Forum. We also accompanied them to Her Majesty's Theatre to see Mickey Katz with his Borscht Belt ensemble and plays such as *My Fair Lady*.

One of our youth projects was to provide sports equipment and entertainment to the Shawbridge Boys' Farm, an institution located in the Laurentians north of Montreal for the rehabilitation of troubled young boys of various denominations. I personally played a role in the rehabilitation of the young people by working with the Honourable George Nicholson in the Montreal youth courthouse, sharing information with the social workers. In another youth project in Verdun, a borough of Montreal, we gave financial assistance to Pastor Johnson for the home he founded for youth with drug problems. And every December, along with Radio c k g m, we helped the Salvation Army collect money for the needy through a telethon in Montreal and delivered food boxes to the poor for the Christmas holidays.

While my associate Joe Kramer was chairman, the Knights also sponsored the Oldtimers' hockey game to raise money for Montreal's social welfare agencies. Our team, comprised of such former famous Montreal Canadiens players as Maurice Richard, Henri Richard,

Boom Boom Geoffrion, Doug Harvey and Dollard Saint-Laurent, played against a team from Detroit.

I was also one of the committee co-chairmen of the annual Diamond Gloves boxing tournament, with the late Dave Aronoff serving as chairman. Professional sportsmen such as George Springate, George Dixon and Red Storey volunteered their time, and sportswear was donated by the YMHA, the Palestre Nationale, a junior hockey team, and the Casa d'Italia community centre. The proceeds were divided among organizations that helped young people get off the streets by giving them the opportunity to learn and play various sports.

As a child of the Holocaust, I, like many other young survivors, was robbed of the opportunity to have a bar mitzvah and I sympathized with the pain and bitterness that disadvantaged Jewish boys in Montreal felt when their friends celebrated their bar mitzvahs with parties and gifts. I wanted to do something about this, so I proposed to Rabbi Frank of the Spanish and Portuguese Synagogue that we hire a teacher to instruct boys who lacked the means to have bar mitzvah lessons on the *maftir* and use the small chapel in his synagogue on Thursday mornings. Rabbi Frank and I knew each other well because he was also the chaplain at the Douglas Hospital in Verdun, where the Knights of Pythias had volunteered, and he agreed to my proposal at once. I took on the task of supplying *tefillin* (phylacteries) and *tallisim* (prayer shawls) through Schreter's clothing store, as well as refreshments and drinks. Thanks to the generosity of the late Rabbi Frank, these bar mitzvahs took place throughout the 1960s.

Following in my father's footsteps, I decided to participate in Jewish institutions as well. In 1955, I became a member of the executive of the Canadian Jewish Congress for the Quebec region, where I was active for many years. I have also been a member of the Chaplaincy Holiday Committee under the umbrella of the Federation Combined Jewish Appeal (CJA), working with Rabbi Wolff and chairman Gerry Weinstein, whom I met at the Knights of Pythias. We all helped to look after twenty-two hospitals and institutions in Montreal where there were Jewish patients, providing them with fruit baskets and other food on Jewish holidays, such as special Passover food and matzah, Chanukah gelt, and *shalach-manos* on Purim. The Knights of Pythias and Rabbi Cohen of the Lubavitch movement supplied us with the items and students from Jewish schools volunteered their time to distribute them.

Since 1985, I have also been a governor for the Inter-Service Club Council, an organization dedicated to the welfare of children. Every December, we organized the Telethon of Stars to raise money for research into children's diseases at the Montreal Children's Hospital, Sainte-Justine Hospital and Laval University. We raised about $4,000,000 a year through the telethon. The governors, myself included, often visited the research labs, as well as the children in hospital.

∿

In 1977, I was lucky enough to meet Patricia Fox on a blind date. She was born in Montreal to Florence and Oscar Fox. We got married in June 1984. She had two children from her first marriage – a son, Randy, who was born in 1962, and a daughter, Judy, born in 1965. Randy and Judy both completed university and now live in Toronto. Randy has two children and is married to Kris. Their eldest son, Joseph, born in 1993, is named after my father, and his middle name is Ian, after my mother, which is extremely meaningful to me. Their second son, Rhys, was born in 1997. Judy and her husband, Andrew, also have two children – a son, Adam, born in 1995, and a daughter, Orion, born in 1999. I am proud and lucky to have such a beautiful family. They are the children I never had and the grandchildren with whom I have been blessed.

∿

In 1992, I was honoured by Ramon Hnatyshyn, governor general of

Canada, with a medal and a certificate that reads, "The Commemorative Medal for the 125th anniversary of the Confederation of Canada is conferred upon Michael Kutz in Recognition of Significant Contribution to Compatriots and Community and to Canada 1967–1992." Six years later, on the occasion of the fiftieth anniversary of the Declaration of Human Rights on November 18, 1998, I was honoured by the Canadian government in Ottawa.

As a Canadian citizen, I share my honours with all the citizens of Canada, and with my wife, Pat, for her energy, time and love, as well as her understanding and support for what I do in the community. My beloved wife has always encouraged me and assisted me in the various projects to which I devote my time and energy.

Through the Knights of Pythias, I was also active in the Israel Bond Organization for a long time, working with national president, Julius Briskin, and the late Chaim Levine. We organized cocktail parties and evening banquets to sell Israel bonds to help strengthen the Israeli economy. Through my love for Israel, concern for its development, and involvement in various projects, I also became active in the Jewish National Fund (JNF), representing the Knights of Pythias and helping to fundraise. I gave a great deal of my time to a telethon drive that took place every year at Tu b'Shvat, a holiday that is dedicated to environmental initiatives. The accomplishments of this organization are almost indescribable but are evident in the work they do to build the country of Israel by planting trees; by constructing parks and avenues and draining swamps to make Israel fertile for the benefit of its entire population; and by helping to settle new immigrants by providing them with housing and jobs.

At the beginning of 1990, the JNF decided to organize a tour of Israel for Tu b'Shvat. With much of the world not supportive of the political situation in Israel, the goal was to bring more tourists to the country. Terrorist groups had caused considerable damage by burning down forests, and Jews in Montreal and other parts of Canada raised money to help to plant new trees. When Pat and I and some of our friends received information about a tour to Israel, it didn't take very long for us to make up our minds to travel there.

The trip was especially important for me because my father's only surviving brother, Shimon, lived in Netanya with his wife, Rachel. Their daughter, Mara, her husband, Gregory, and their three children, Baruch, Karen and Osnat, lived in Herzliya. I can't remember the names of my father's other siblings who had lived in Rovno, Ludwipol, Sarny and Korets – they all perished in the Holocaust. During the war, Rachel survived in Leningrad, participating in the defence of the city during the lengthy German siege. My uncle Shimon, who had been repeatedly honoured for his bravery when he fought in the Red Army on several fronts during the war, was labelled a *refusenik* years after the war because he had applied to the Soviet government for a visa to leave the country and immigrate to Israel. Emigration from the Soviet Union was very restricted for Jews at the time. My uncle was immediately fired from his job as an electronic engineer and he was arrested and sent to Siberia for ten years of hard labour. He was sent to the same camp where activist, former *refusenik* and future Israeli politician Anatoly, now Natan, Sharansky was imprisoned. At some point in the 1980s, after several years in the camp, Uncle Shimon was released and given five days to leave the country with his wife, daughter and son-in-law, who had all been granted permission to leave with him. I'm not sure why, but for some reason he couldn't travel under the name Kutz, so the passport he was issued listed his last name as Rotenberg. After surviving the difficult war years and the gulag, he and his family finally arrived in Israel.

On Wednesday, February 7, 1990, about 750 participants from Ottawa, Montreal, Toronto and Winnipeg left Mirabel and Pearson airports to fly to Israel to participate in this very special JNF Mission Tour. Among them were Mrs. Neri Bloomfield, national president of the JNF Canada; Morris Zilka, vice president of the JNF; and Israel's ambassador to Canada, His Excellency Israel Gur-Arieh, and his wife, Shulamit.

We arrived on two El Al airplanes on Thursday, February 8, at 2:00 p.m. at Ben Gurion International Airport, where Moshe Arens, minister for foreign affairs, and His Excellency James K. Bartleman, Canadian ambassador to Israel, welcomed us and wished us a successful tour. We all received flowers from young schoolchildren and four school bands played music for us as we sang along and danced the hora, the traditional folk dance. It was such a momentous occasion that we all had tears in our eyes. After our greeting, seventeen buses waited to take us to the Western Wall in Jerusalem. Pat and I, along with Gerry and Lynn Weinstein and our other friends, were assigned to bus No. 17.

Completely unbeknownst to me, my friend and fellow Pythian Gerry Weinstein, as well as the JNF, had planned an unbelievable surprise for me. As the buses drove away from the airport, the tour guides in all the other sixteen buses announced that the bar mitzvah of child survivor Michael Kutz would be taking place at the Kotel, the Western Wall, the holy wall in Jerusalem. Some of the people who heard the announcement knew me, such as my good friends Joe and Sylvia Greenstone, so needless to say, they were shocked. The news was not announced on my bus, and everyone managed to keep the secret.

We arrived at the Kotel later that afternoon. Everyone rushed to the holy wall and Lieutenant-Colonel Perez came over and told me to hurry along with him, so as not to be late for a religious ceremony. Then a young rabbi dressed in a *kapote*, a beautiful black coat, ran up to me and took me by the arm, telling me to come quickly. I asked him where they were taking me. The rabbi answered that my bar mitzvah, which could not take place in the sorrowful days of the German occupation, was going to be celebrated here at the Kotel. They led me to a table with a Torah scroll on it, surrounded by people from the tour. Lieutenant-Colonel Perez announced that this historic occasion was the bar mitzvah of Michael Kutz, who had helped celebrate so many bar mitzvahs for Jewish orphans and boys from disadvantaged homes in Montreal. The time had come for everyone present to take part in his bar mitzvah at the holiest place in Jewish history, a monument to the Jewish people, a people that live and breathe in their own free country, Israel.

The Lubavitch rabbi brought over a *tallis* and *tefillin* that had been sent two days earlier from New York, where they had been blessed by the beloved Lubavitcher Rebbe. At that moment, tears fell from my eyes as I looked at the great holy wall, with its holy stones. During the ceremony, my legs felt weak, my face broke into a sweat and I began to tremble. I thought of the war years, of losing my parents, my brother and my sisters to the Nazis, along with our large extended family. I thought of all the Jews of Nieśwież, and the six million Jewish martyrs, among them 1.5 million children, whose lives had been cut short in ghettos, crematoria, slave labour camps, and by hunger and disease. I, a child survivor, was standing in this holy place as a symbol of the Jewish people, representing them all and promising that we would never forget them. They live on in our hearts, our thoughts and our souls.

The people in our group who participated in my celebration were also very emotional, weeping tears of joy as they helped read from the Torah. When the service ended, people sang and danced the hora, pulling me into the circle. It was an incredibly meaningful experience. Later, we briefly visited the Moriah Gardens Hotel and then went to the Hilton hotel, where a delegation from the Jewish National Fund told us that there would be a special dinner that evening.

When I entered the hall at 7:00 p.m., I found tables covered in beautiful tablecloths with flowers on them and complimentary bottles of Israeli wine from the hotel management. The master of ceremonies was Lieutenant-Colonel Perez, who was assisted by Morris Zilka and Rabbi Meyer Krentzman. On the stage in front of my table was a cake at least a metre and a half long on which was written "Mazel tov Michael on your Bar Mitzvah." Pat and I lit the first candle, and my friends from Montreal lit the rest. I cut the cake and everyone in the room was served a piece. I was then presented with a special scroll on which was inscribed, "The Jewish National Fund of Canada hereby proclaims Michael Kutz of Montreal, Quebec, Canada as a Chai Jerusalemite on the occasion of his Bar Mitzvah at the Kotel in Jerusalem, February 8, 1990, and in so doing, places his name on the Wall of Honour in Ramot Park inscribed therein for eternity by Lynn and Gerry Weinstein, the Kutz family and friends, and Neri Bloomfield, President of the JNF Canada." As long as I live, I shall never forget everything that was done for me that day and evening.

~

On Saturday morning, Pat and I went to Netanya to visit my uncle Shimon, aunt Rachel, and my cousins Mara, Gregory and their children. It was the first time that I had ever met them; it was such a joyous occasion. We told each other about our lives and experiences, especially the difficult journeys we had each taken to survive World War II and finally meet across a distance of thousands of miles. My wife was immediately adopted by all of them as though she were their own child. For me, it was the first time since the Holocaust that I had rediscovered such close family. During my time in Israel I saw them often and to this day we have a very close relationship.

The next morning, our group went to take part in a ceremony to plant trees in Canada Park near Moshav Neve Ilan. One hundred children from various schools in Israel had also come to plant trees, and a youth orchestra and a choir entertained everyone. The guest of honour was the president of the State of Israel, His Excellency Chaim Herzog, who explained the holiday of Tu b'Shvat, which symbolizes the bond between Jews and the State of Israel. He pointed out where terrorists had set fire to the forests, destroying all the trees that had contributed so much to the country's ecology. The president called upon those of us who were visitors to help build the country by making a contribution toward the cost of absorbing the thousands of people who were anxious to settle in Israel and once again be part of the

Jewish people. The Canadian ambassador to Israel, His Excellency James K. Bartleman, assured us of Canada's unwavering support for Israel's security and the broadening of relations between the two countries, adding that he was pleased to meet such a large group of Canadian citizens visiting Israel.

That same day, we visited the *Scrolls of Fire*, the Holocaust monument by sculptor Nathan Rapoport. Situated in the JNF-KKL (Keren Kayemeth LeIsrael) Martyrs Forest in the hills around Jerusalem, the monument depicts Jewish history over the years of exile up to the Holocaust, the greatest catastrophe to befall the Jewish people.

The next place we visited was Yad Vashem, Israel's memorial and world-renowned research centre that documents the Holocaust through written material, photographs and exhibits. Going through the children's pavilion in darkness, with candles giving the impression of a sky lit by millions of tiny stars, and hearing the names of the children read out one by one through a loudspeaker, we all felt bitter and depressed. Anyone with a conscience cannot fathom what they are seeing here. Yad Vashem stands as a monument both to the past and to our hope for a different future. Outside, on the exterior walls, are inscribed the names of the Righteous Among the Nations – European gentiles who risked their own lives and the lives of their families to hide and protect Jews. Their humanity and generosity will never be forgotten. As we walked through the exhibits, we stopped to watch slides of the Jewish fighters in the ghettos and Jewish partisans in the forests of occupied Europe. Surprisingly, one of the slides was a photograph of me with the twelve other surviving Jews from my town in front of the burned-out Kalte Synagogue, where the first uprising against the Nazis had taken place in the summer of 1942. The picture made a huge impact on me and my whole group. The next day, I received a copy of the photograph from Yad Vashem.

A few days after our visit to Yad Vashem, we visited the fortress of Masada. We ascended to the top of the mountain by cable car and on narrow steps. I had read books and had seen television programs about the Jews' historic struggle against the Romans in Masada. It was very emotional being there, seeing all the archaeological finds and knowing that this was where our people had heroically fought to the last person, refusing to surrender to the Romans. Milton Winston, a producer from Montreal, had his camera crew photograph the fortress and interview me and my wife, some of which was later broadcast on television in Montreal and Toronto.

Over the course of our thirteen-day trip we visited the entire country, from the Sea of Galilee to the Dead Sea. We were all enchanted with the beauty of the small State of Israel. Our group became one big family, sharing with one another all we had learned and the wonders we had seen. The tour will remain in my memory forever.

∼

On my return to Montreal, I became very active in the Montreal Holocaust Centre. I started speaking to schoolchildren from all over Montreal and Quebec, as well as to high school students who come to visit the centre from places like Vermont, Boston, Toronto and other cities in Ontario. I have chosen to speak mainly to the non-Jewish schools because the Holocaust is something new to these students and they are curious to learn about it. They are fascinated when I tell them how I, as a ten-year-old boy, escaped from a mass grave and was hidden for six months by a Polish-Catholic family, and how I reached the dense Belorussian forests and became a partisan to take revenge for the murder of so many of my people.

I also played an active part in the March of the Living, an annual event in which thousands of Jewish students from different countries travel to Poland to visit the death camps, most notably Auschwitz-Birkenau. They also visit cities and towns where Jews had lived for hundreds of years before the war. The students are given seminars ahead of time to prepare them both physically and psychologically for what they are about to see, and I talked to them about my history and the history of Jewish life in Poland. The students asked many serious questions about the past and about the destruction of the Jewish people in Europe. They learned a great deal about the heroic ghetto uprising in Warsaw as well as resistance in other towns and cities. They also knew about the partisans in the forests, but this was often the first time that they met a child survivor. I received hundreds of letters from young people who visited the exhibits and heard me speak. They all say that they admire my heroism as a child partisan who was determined to survive.

I tell my story to the world and to young people in Canada because I feel an obligation to keep the legacy alive for future generations, to be vigilant so that the Holocaust never happens again, to recognize the rights of all peoples regardless of colour, religion or nationality, and to live together and respect one another because we are all God's children.

I wish to personally thank Canada for giving me the opportunity to live in a free country. I consider myself one of the lucky ones, for I was able to rebuild my life in a free and democratic country like Canada – a wonderful place in which to live. As for my involvement in the community, what I have done over the years is not unique. Many of us, the child survivors, share the same values of "giving back to the community." May God grant me good health so that I may continue my involvement for many years to come.

Glossary

Aktion (German; pl. *Aktionen*) The brutal roundup of Jews for forced labour, forcible resettlement into ghettos, mass murder by shooting or deportation to death camps.

Allied Zones of Germany The four zones that Germany was divided into after its defeat in World War II, each administered by one of the four major Allied powers – the United States, Britain, France and the Soviet Union. These administrative zones existed in Germany between 1945 and 1949.

American Jewish Joint Distribution Committee (JDC) Also known colloquially as the "Joint." A charitable organization that provided material support for persecuted Jews in Germany and other Nazi-occupied territories and facilitated their emigration to neutral countries such as Portugal, Turkey and China. Between 1939 and 1944, JDC officials helped close to 81,000 European Jews find asylum in various parts of the world. Between 1944 and 1947, the JDC assisted more than 100,000 refugees living in DP camps by offering retraining programs, cultural activities and financial assistance for emigration.

Anders' Army The informal name for the Polish Armed Forces in the East that was led by General Władysław Anders (1892–1970) between 1941 and 1946. General Anders, a cavalry commander, was taken prisoner by Soviet forces during the invasion of Poland in September 1939. In June 1941, after Germany invaded the Soviet Union, Anders was released by the Soviets to establish an armed force of exiled Poles living in the USSR to assist the Red Army in its fight against Germany. By 1942 this force included approximately 72,000 combatants – among them between 4,000 and 5,000 Jews. In August 1942, political tensions between Soviet authorities and the Polish government-in-exile, as well as short-ages of equipment and rations, led Anders to redeploy his forces to the Middle East. There, he formed the Second Corps of the Polish Armed Forces. From 1943 to 1946 Anders and his men fought alongside the British forces in Italy. After the war, Anders was stripped of his citizenship by Poland's Communist regime. He remained exiled in London until his death in 1970.

Anschluss (German; literally, connection) The de facto annexation of Austria into Greater Germany by the Nazi regime in 1938. When Austrian Chancellor Kurt Schuschnigg announced a plebiscite on the question of Austrian annexation (*Anschluss*), he was sub-sequently pressured into cancelling the plebiscite and forced to resign. When President Wilhelm Miklas refused to appoint Aus-trian Nazi leader Arthur Seyss-Inquart to replace Schuschnigg, Germany invaded Austria on March 12, 1938. The enthusiastic reception the German forces received from the Austrian popula-tion gave Hitler the cover to annex Austria outright on March 13. The German army marched in to solidify the annexation and a Nazi-controlled plebiscite held under strict Nazi supervision on April 10 was 99.7 per cent in favour of the *Anschluss*. Austria was renamed Ostmark and ceased to exist as a separate nation until 1945.

antisemitism Prejudice, discrimination, persecution and/or hatred against Jewish people, institutions, culture and symbols.

aron-koydesh (Yiddish; Holy Ark) The place in a synagogue where the Torah scrolls are kept.

Attlee, Clement (1883–1967) The British Labour Party leader from 1935 to 1955 and prime minister of the United Kingdom between 1945 and 1951. Attlee followed the pro-Arab policy of foreign secretary Ernest Bevin regarding British Mandate Palestine. Although he publicly declared the Mandate unworkable in February 1947, his government continued to preside over British Mandate Palestine until Britain's official withdrawal on May 14, 1948. *See also* Bevin, Ernest; British Mandate Palestine.

bar mitzvah (Hebrew; literally, one to whom commandments apply) The age of thirteen when, according to Jewish tradition, boys become religiously and morally responsible for their actions and are considered adults for the purpose of synagogue ritual. A bar mitzvah is also the synagogue ceremony and family celebration that mark the attainment of this status, during which the boy is called upon to read a portion of the Torah and recite the prescribed prayers in a public prayer forum. In the latter half of the twentieth century, liberal Jews instituted an equivalent ceremony and celebration for girls – called a bat mitzvah.

Begin, Menachem (1913–1992) Israeli politician who was prime minister from 1977 to 1983. During the 1930s, Begin was a prominent member of the Zionist Betar youth movement in Poland, which led to his arrest by Soviet authorities in 1940 and his subsequent internment in a labour camp in north Russia until 1941. Upon his release, he joined Anders' Army, and while stationed in British Mandate Palestine, he left the army in 1942 to join the Irgun – a paramilitary organization that opposed British rule in Palestine, which he commanded until 1948. During the 1960s and 1970s, Begin led the opposition parties in Israel's parliament and became prime minister in 1977. In 1978, he and Egyptian president Anwar el-Sadat were awarded the Nobel Peace Prize for the signing of the Camp David Accords that led to a peace treaty between Egypt and Israel. *See also* Anders' Army; Betar; British Mandate Palestine; Irgun.

beis din (Hebrew; house of judgement) A rabbinical court of Judaism that has jurisdiction over certain religious matters, such as conversions to Judaism.

Belorussian Headquarters of the Partisan Movement The Soviet-controlled organization created in September 1942 that was subordinate to Stalin's Central Staff of the Partisan Movement, which was established in May 1942 to coordinate and control partisan resistance against the Nazis. Under Stalin's command, the Belorussian Headquarters of the Partisan Movement supported the Red Army's fight against Nazi Germany. The partisan movement, which had previously lacked directive and a central command, now had organized partisan staff in each Soviet republic. The staff had a structure similar to that of the Red Army, subdivided into sections that included intelligence operations, supplies, transportation and political security, which were connected through a central radio communications network. *See also* partisan; Stalin, Joseph.

Bereza Kartuska A town in Poland where a detention camp was created in 1934 to hold people that the Polish state viewed as opponents to the regime, such as communists and Ukrainian nationalists. The prison closed in September 1939; the staff abandoned it when they learned of the Soviet invasion of Poland.

Betar A Zionist youth movement founded by Revisionist Zionist leader Ze'ev Jabotinsky in 1923 that encouraged the development of a new generation of Zionist activists based on the ideals of courage, self-respect, military training, defence of Jewish life and property, and settlement in Israel to establish a Jewish state in British Mandate Palestine. In 1934, Betar membership in Poland numbered more than 40,000. During the 1930s and 1940s, as antisemitism increased and the Nazis launched their murderous campaign against the Jews of Europe, Betar rescued thousands of Jews by organizing illegal immigration to British Mandate Palestine. The Betar movement today, closely aligned with Israel's right-wing Likud party, remains involved in supporting Jewish and Zionist activism around the world.

Bevin, Ernest (1881–1951) British Labour Party politician who was foreign secretary of the United Kingdom from 1945 to 1951. With regard to Britain's mandate in Palestine, Bevin adopted a pro-Arab stance, not yielding to post-war pressure to change Britain's restrictive immigration policies against Jews, regardless of the plight of the hundreds of thousands of Jewish displaced persons after the war. The British mandate was withdrawn on May 14, 1948, when the State of Israel was declared. *See also* British Mandate Palestine.

Bielski, Tuvia (1906–1987) The Jewish resistance leader of a large Jewish partisan group during World War II that came to be known as the Bielski Partisans. In 1942, Tuvia Bielski and his brothers Alexander, Asael and Aharon set up a mobile camp in the forests of western Belarus with the prime objective of protecting Jews from the Nazi occupation. By the end of 1943, the partisan group, which had grown to 1,200, had settled deep in the Naliboki forest and operated a "family camp" as a small, multi-generational community complete with a kitchen, bakery, mill, tannery, school and synagogue. Tuvia Bielski is credited with saving the lives of the Jews in his partisan detachment.

bimah (Hebrew) The raised platform in a synagogue from which the Torah is read.

Blyukher, Vasily (1889–1938) Soviet military commander who was suspected of espionage during Joseph Stalin's rule and convicted during Stalin's "purges" in October 1938. Blyukher was never formally tried and the circumstances of his death remain unknown, although it was officially confirmed in 1956. *See also* Stalin, Joseph.

Bricha (Hebrew; literally, escape) The name given to the massive, organized, clandestine migration of Jews from eastern Europe and Displaced Persons camps to pre-state Israel following World War II. Estimates of the number of Jews helped by Bricha range from 80,000 to 250,000.

British Broadcasting Corporation (BBC) The British public service broadcaster. During World War II, the BBC broadcast radio programming to Europe in German and the languages of the occupied countries. Allied forces used some of this programming to send coded messages to resistance groups. It was illegal to listen to these broadcasts, but many people in Nazi-occupied Europe turned to it as the most reliable source of news.

British Mandate Palestine The area of the Middle East under British rule from 1923 to 1948, as established by the League of Nations after World War I. During that time, the United Kingdom severely restricted Jewish immigration. The Mandate area encompassed present-day Israel, Jordan, the West Bank and the Gaza Strip.

Bukharian Jews The Jewish population from the Central Asian region previously called the Emirate of Bukhara (1785–1920), which encompassed Uzbekistan, Tajikistan and Kyrgyzstan. Bukharian, or Bukharan, Jews speak the Persian-Tajik dialect Bukhori, which includes elements of Hebrew, and follow Sephardic customs. *See also* Sephardic.

Canadian Jewish Congress (CJC) An advocacy organization and lobbying group for the Canadian Jewish community from 1919 to 2011. In 1947, the CJC convinced the Canadian government to re-issue Privy Council Order 1647 – originally adopted in 1942 to admit five hundred Jewish refugee children from Vichy France, although they never made it out – that allowed for one thousand Jewish children under the age of eighteen to be admitted to Canada. Under the auspices of the CJC, who would provide for the refugees' care, the War Orphans Project was established in April 1947 and the CJC began searching for Jewish war orphans with the help of the United Nations Relief and Rehabilitation Administration (UNRRA). Between 1947 and 1949, 1,123 young Jewish refugees came to Canada. The CJC was restructured in 2007 and its functions subsumed under the Centre for Israel and Jewish Affairs (CIJA) in 2011. *See also* United Nations Relief and Rehabilitation Administration (UNRRA).

Carabinieri (Italian; cavalry soldier) The military police force of Italy.

Catherine the Great (1729–1796) Also known as Catherine II. Catherine the Great was the Empress of Russia from 1762 until her death and is renowned for creating a stronger and expanded empire.

Central Command. *See* Belorussian Headquarters of the Partisan Movement.

Central Committee of the Communist Party (Soviet Union) The highest body of the Communist Party of the Soviet Union, the committee managed all Communist Party affairs between Party Congresses. In 1942, the Central Committee was responsible for establishing the Central Staff of the Partisan Movement. *See also* Belorussian Headquarters of the Partisan Movement.

Chamberlain, Neville (1869–1940) The British politician who was prime minister of the United Kingdom from 1937 to 1940, Chamberlain is most well known for declaring that he had achieved "peace for our time" by signing the September 1938 Munich Pact ceding control of the Sudetenland to Nazi Germany. Although Chamberlain hoped this negotiation would avert war, Germany invaded Poland less than a year later, precipitating the start of World War II. As required by the August 1939 Polish-British Common Defense Pact that guaranteed the defense of Poland in the event of an invasion, both the United Kingdom and France declared war on Germany. Neither country, however, directly came to Poland's aid during the German invasion on September 1, 1939.

Chanukah (also Hanukah; Hebrew; dedication) An eight-day festival celebrated in December to mark the victory of the Jews against foreign conquerors who desecrated the Temple in Jerusalem in the second century BCE. Traditionally, each night of the festival is marked by lighting an eight-branch candelabrum called a menorah to commemorate the rededication of the Temple and the miracle of its lamp burning for eight days without oil.

cheder (Hebrew; literally, room) An Orthodox Jewish elementary school that teaches the fundamentals of Jewish religious observance and textual study, as well as the Hebrew language.

chevra kadisha (Aramaic; literally, holy society) Jewish burial society. An organization comprised of Jewish volunteers that helps
prepare the body for burial according to Jewish ritual and law.

Chumash (Hebrew) The Pentateuch. The term is used to refer to the
Five Books of Moses when they are in book form, as distinct from
the Torah scrolls.

chuppah (Hebrew; literally, covering) The canopy used in traditional Jewish weddings that is usually made of a cloth (sometimes a
prayer shawl) stretched or supported over four poles. It is meant
to symbolize the home the couple will build together.

Commissar A Communist Party official assigned to Soviet army
units to assure adherence to Party principles and ensure Party
loyalty. At different times in the USSR's history, the role of the
commissars was very powerful, allowing them to operate outside
the military hierarchy and report directly to Party leaders. Political commissars were vital in boosting morale among the troops
by reinforcing Communist party ideology and preventing dissen-
sion in the ranks.

displaced persons (DPs) People who find themselves homeless and
stateless at the end of a war. Following World War II, millions of
people, especially European Jews, found that they had no homes
to return to or that it was unsafe to do so. To resolve the staggering
refugee crisis that resulted, Allied authorities and the United Nations Relief and Rehabilitation Administration (UNRRA) established Displaced Persons (DP) camps to provide temporary shelter and assistance to refugees, and help them transition towards
resettlement. *See also* DP camps.

DP camps Facilities set up by the Allied authorities and the United
Nations Relief and Rehabilitation Administration (UNRRA) in
October 1945 to resolve the refugee crisis that arose at the end
of World War II. The camps provided temporary shelter and assistance to the millions of people – not only Jews – who had been
displaced from their home countries as a result of the war and

helped them prepare for resettlement. Michael Kutz was one of approximately 30,000 Jewish DPs who entered Italy between September 1946 and June 1948. Italy, which eventually set up about twenty-five DP camps to house refugees, was the main transit point for Jews to reach British Mandate Palestine. *See also* British Mandate Palestine; United Nations Relief and Rehabilitation Administration (UNRRA).

Einsatzgruppen (German) Mobile death squads responsible for the rounding up and murder of Jews in mass shooting operations. They were a key component in the implementation of the Nazis' so-called Final Solution in eastern Europe.

Eisenhower, Dwight D. (1890–1969) General in the United States Army, Supreme Commander of Allied Forces during World War II and president of the United States between 1953 and 1961. Eisenhower was responsible for planning the invasion of Normandy, France on June 6, 1944 that marked the beginning of the liberation of western Europe during World War II. *See also* Montgomery, Bernard.

Endeks (in Polish, *Endecja*) An antisemitic political party, also known as the Nationalist Democrats, that was led by Polish politician Roman Dmowski (1864–1939) in interwar Poland. The party advocated for boycotts of Jewish businesses, a redistribution of wealth from Jews to Poles and Jewish emigration from Poland.

Eretz Yisrael (Hebrew) The biblical Land of Israel.

Farband (Yiddish; literally, alliance; abbreviation of Yiddish Natzionaler Arbeiter Farband; in English, Jewish National Workers Alliance) A Zionist welfare organization established in 1910 that was affiliated with the Labour Zionist movement in the United States. It focused on Jewish workers' rights and providing insurance and benefits. In 1980, the organization's name was changed to the Labour Zionist Alliance of Canada, although many people continued to refer to it by its original Yiddish name, the Farband.

Four Questions The questions that are recited at the start of the Passover seder, usually by the youngest child at the table. As much of the seder is designed to fulfill the biblical obligation to tell the Exodus story to children, the ritual of asking the Four Questions is one of the most important at the seder. The questions revolve around the theme of how this night of commemoration of the Exodus is different from other nights – e.g., Why do we eat un-leavened bread? Why do we eat bitter herbs? The readings that follow answer the questions and in doing so tell the Exodus story. *See also* seder; Passover.

General Jewish Labour Bund (in Yiddish, Algemeyner Yidisher Arbeter Bund in Lite, Polyn, un Rusland; in English, the Jew-ish Workers' Alliance in Lithuania, Poland and Russia) A Jewish social-democratic revolutionary movement founded in Vilnius, Lithuania in 1897 to fight for the rights of the Yiddish-speaking Jewish worker in Eastern Europe, advocate Jewish cultural auton-omy in the Diaspora and champion Yiddish language and secular culture. In interwar Poland, the Bund served as one of many Jew-ish political organizations that also had affiliated schools, youth groups and sports clubs.

General Zionists A term initially used to indicate membership in one of the nationwide sections of the Zionist Organization – later the World Zionist Organization – as opposed to any of the smaller Zionist factions with specific political affiliation. As the Zionist movement became increasingly polarized between Labour Zion-ism on the left and Revisionist Zionism on the right, in 1922, the non-aligned mainstream Zionists formed the Organization of General Zionists as a centrist political party within the Zionist Organization and, after 1949 and the creation of the state of Israel, participated in elections for the Knesset, Israel's elected parlia-ment. *See also* Zionism; Zionist and Jewish movements in inter-war Poland.

Gestapo (German; abbreviation of Geheime Staatspolizei, the Secret State Police of Nazi Germany) The Gestapo was the brutal force that dealt with the perceived enemies of the Nazi regime and was responsible for rounding up European Jews for deportation to the death camps. They operated with very few legal constraints and were also responsible for issuing exit visas to the residents of German-occupied areas. A number of Gestapo members also joined the Einsatzgruppen, the mobile killing squads responsible for the roundup and murder of Jews in eastern Poland and the USSR through mass shooting operations.

ghetto A confined residential area for Jews. The term originated in Venice, Italy in 1516 with a law requiring all Jews to live on a segregated, gated island known as Ghetto Nuovo. Throughout the Middle Ages in Europe, Jews were often forcibly confined to gated Jewish neighbourhoods. During the Holocaust, the Nazis forced Jews to live in crowded and unsanitary conditions in rundown districts of cities and towns.

g'milas chasodim (Hebrew; literally, acts of loving kindness) An agency that offers interest-free loans to those in need.

Gordonia A Zionist youth movement founded in Poland in 1925 that promoted immigration to pre-state Israel. *See also* Zionist and Jewish movements in interwar Poland.

grager (Yiddish; rattle) A noise-making device traditionally used during the holiday of Purim at the mention of the name "Haman" during the telling of the Purim story. *See also* Purim.

Grynszpan, Herschel (1921– exact date unknown) A German-Jewish immigrant in France who killed German embassy official Ernst vom Rath on November 7, 1938. Grynszpan stated that his intent was to protest the conditions for Polish-born Jews in Germany – he had heard from his family about the persecution of the 12,000 Polish-born Jews who were arrested and expelled from their residences in October 1938. The Nazis used the killing of vom Rath as an excuse to initiate the Kristallnacht pogrom in Germany and Austria a few days later. After his arrest, Herschel Grynszpan was incarcerated in the Flossenbürg and Sachsenhausen concentration camps. The date of his death is unknown, but assumed to be between 1943 and 1945. *See also* Kristallnacht.

Gymnasium (German) A word used throughout central and eastern Europe to mean high school.

Gypsies The term for the Sinti and Roma people commonly used in the past, and now generally considered to be derogatory. The Sinti and Roma are a nomadic people who speak Romani, an Indo-European language. During the Holocaust, which the Roma refer to in Romani as the *Porajmos* – the devouring – they were stripped of their citizenship under the Nuremberg Laws and were targeted for death under Hitler's race policies. In Auschwitz-Birkenau, more than 20,000 Sinti and Roma were segregated into the "Gypsy camp" and then systematically murdered. The estimation of how many Roma were killed during World War II varies widely and has been difficult to document – estimations generally range from between 200,000 to one million.

hachshara (Hebrew; literally, preparation) A training program to prepare new immigrants for life in the Land of Israel.

Haftorah The portion read from the Book of Prophets after the Torah reading at Sabbath services and major festivals; it is traditionally sung by the youth who is celebrating his or her bar/bat mitzvah.

Haganah (Hebrew; The Defense) The Jewish paramilitary force in British Mandate Palestine that existed from 1920 to 1948 and later became the Israel Defense Forces. After World War II, there were branches of the Haganah in the DP camps in Europe, and members helped coordinate illegal immigration to British Mandate Palestine. *See also* DP camps; Irgun.

hakafot (Hebrew; literally, circles) The seven circuitous dances performed while holding the Torah during the celebratory holiday of Simchat Torah. *See also* Simchat Torah.

halutz (Hebrew; pioneer) Agricultural immigrants who moved to pre-state Israel to help clear the land, plant trees and drain marshes to establish settlements and build self-sustaining communities.

Halutzim are primarily associated with the wave of immigration known as the Third Aliyah (1919–1923) that followed in the wake of World War I and the establishment of the British Mandate in Palestine.

Hashomer Hatzair (Hebrew) The Youth Guard. A left-wing Zionist youth movement founded in Central Europe in 1913 to prepare young Jews to become workers and farmers, to establish kibbutzim – collective settlements – in pre-state Israel and work the land as pioneers. Before World War II, there were 70,000 Hashomer Hatzair members worldwide and many of those in Nazi-occupied territories led resistance activities in the ghettos and concentration camps or joined partisan groups in the forests of east-central Europe. It is the oldest Zionist youth movement still in existence. *See also* Zionism.

Hatikvah (Hebrew; literally, the hope) A poem composed by Naphtali Herz Imber in 1878 that was set to a folk melody and adopted as their anthem by early Zionist groups in Europe, including the First Zionist Congress in 1897. When the State of Israel was established in 1948, it was unofficially proclaimed the national anthem; it officially became so in 2004.

hekdesh (Hebrew; consecrated property) A historical term that originally meant the dedication of property for the Temple and later denoted the property set aside for charitable works or dedicated to helping the poor.

Herzl, Theodor (1860–1904) Austro-Hungarian journalist who wrote about the need to combat antisemitism by establishing a Jewish state in the homeland of Biblical Israel. Herzl is credited as the founder of Zionism. *See also* Zionism.

Heydrich, Reinhard (1904–1942) Chief of the Reich Main Security Office (overseeing both the SD, the Nazi intelligence service, and the Gestapo) and one of the orchestrators of the "Final Solution," the Nazi plan for the systematic murder of Europe's Jewish population. While serving as Reichsprotektor of Czechoslovakia,

Heydrich's brutality toward Czech citizens earned him the nickname the "Butcher of Prague." In May 1942, two Czech patriots parachuted in from Britain and attacked Heydrich in Prague by throwing a grenade into his open car; he succumbed to his injuries one week later.

Hilfsverein (German) Aid association.

Histadrut (Hebrew; abbreviation of HaHistadrut HaKlalit shel Ha-Ovdim B'Eretz Yisrael; in English, General Federation of Labourers in the Land of Israel) A labour union established in pre-state Israel in 1920. A branch was established in Montreal in 1943.

Internationale A well-known and widely sung left-wing anthem. Adopted by the socialist movement in the late nineteenth century, it was the de facto national anthem of the Soviet Union until 1944 and is still sung by left-wing groups to this day.

Irgun (abbreviated from Irgun Zvai Le'umi; Hebrew; National Military Organization) The Irgun (also known as the Etzel, its Hebrew acronym) was formed in 1937 after it separated from the Haganah, a paramilitary organization operating in British Mandate Palestine between 1920 and 1948. Due to the increasing level of violence between Arab and Jewish citizens, the Irgun, under the leadership of Revisionist Zionist Ze'ev Jabotinsky, advocated active and armed resistance (in opposition to the policy of restraint that was advocated by the Haganah) as well as the establishment of a Jewish state in Palestine. The Irgun was responsible for numerous attacks in British Mandate Palestine and was also fundamental to the illegal transport and immigration of thousands of European Jews into pre-state Israel. The activities of the Irgun were controversial – some people viewed them as a terrorist organization, while others applauded their efforts as freedom fighters. *See also* Haganah.

Jewish Anti-Fascist Committee (JAFC) A group established by Soviet authorities in April 1942 to drum up political and material support for the Soviet struggle against Nazi Germany from Jewish communities in the West. Solomon Mikhoels, popular actor and director of the Moscow Jewish State Theatre, was appointed chair-man, and the committee had its own Yiddish-language news-paper, *Eynikayt* (Unity). In 1943, Solomon Mikhoels and writer Itzik Feffer raised millions of dollars for the U S S R 's war effort on a seven-month official tour of North America and Great Britain. After the war, the J A F C became a focal point for Soviet Jews and planned to publish a "black book" that documented the Nazis' anti-Jewish crimes. This contradicted official Soviet policy that Nazi atrocities were committed against all Soviet citizens, with no specific reference to Jews. As the situation for Soviet Jews sharply deteriorated in 1948 and an ideological campaign of persecution ramped up, J A F C members became targets of the Soviet regime. Mikhoels was murdered in November 1948 and other members were arrested, tried and executed in purges over the next four years.

Jewish Brigade A battalion formed in September 1944 under the command of the British Eighth Army. The Jewish Brigade includ-ed more than 5,000 volunteers from Palestine. After the war, the Brigade was essential in helping Jewish refugees and organizing their entry into Palestine. It was disbanded by the British in 1946.

Jewish National Fund (in Hebrew, Keren Kayemet LeIsrael) A non-profit organization founded in 1901 to buy, lease and develop the land of pre-state Israel. The Jewish National Fund's projects cur-rently include water conservation, land development and planting trees, of which more than 240 million have been planted since its inception.

Judenrat (German; pl. *Judenräte*) Jewish Council. A group of Jew-ish leaders appointed by the Germans to administer and provide services to the local Jewish population under occupation and carry out German orders. The *Judenräte*, which appeared to be self-governing entities but were actually under complete German control, faced difficult and complex moral decisions under brutal conditions and remain a contentious subject. The chairmen had

114 IF, BY MIRACLE

to decide whether to comply or refuse to comply with German demands. Some were killed by the Nazis for refusing, while others committed suicide. Jewish officials who advocated compliance thought that cooperation might save at least some Jews. Some who denounced resistance efforts did so because they believed that armed resistance would bring death to the entire community.

Kamenev, Lev (1883–1936) Soviet-Jewish Bolshevik politician who was a leading member of the Communist Party from 1917 to 1934. During this time, Kamenev was expelled from the Party three times for various oppositional acts, which culminated in his 1934 arrest for alleged conspiracy in the murder of prominent Communist Sergei Kirov. Along with colleague Grigory Zinoviev and fourteen others, Kamenev was a victim of Stalin's infamous show trials and was executed on August 25, 1936. *See also* Stalin, Joseph; Zinoviev, Grigory.

kibbutz (Hebrew) A collectively owned farm or settlement in Israel democratically governed by its members.

Kielce pogrom The July 1946 riots in a city in Poland where about 250 Jews lived after the war (the pre-war Jewish population had been over 20,000). After the false report of a young Polish boy kidnapped by Jews, police arrested and beat Jewish residents in the city, inciting a mob of hundreds of Polish civilians to violently attack and kill forty Jews while police stood by. Combined with other post-war antisemitic incidents throughout Poland – other pogroms occurred in Rzeszów, Krakow, Tarnów and Sosnowiec, and robberies and blackmail were common – this event was the catalyst for a mass exodus of Jews from Poland; between July 1945 and September 1946, more than 80,000 Jews left Poland.

Knights of Pythias A fraternal organization founded in Washington, DC in 1864 whose motto is "Friendship, Charity, Benevolence."

Komsomol (Russian; abbreviation of Kommunisticheskiy Soyuz Molodyozhi; in English, Communist Union of Youth) The youth movement of the Soviet Communist Party established in 1918 and geared toward youths between fourteen and twenty-eight. The Komsomol mainly functioned as a means of transmitting Party values to future members. Members were frequently favoured over non-members for scholarships and employment; becoming a young officer in Komsomol was often seen as a good way to rise in the Party ranks.

Kristallnacht (German; literally, Night of Broken Glass) A series of pogroms that took place in Germany and Austria between November 9 and 10, 1938. Over the course of twenty-four hours, ninety-one Jews were murdered, 25,000–30,000 were arrested and deported to concentration camps, two hundred synagogues were destroyed and thousands of Jewish businesses and homes were ransacked. Planned by the Nazis as a coordinated attack on the Jews of Germany and Austria, Kristallnacht is often seen as an important turning point in Hitler's policies of systematic persecution of Jews. *See also* Grynszpan, Herschel.

Krylov, Ivan (1769–1844) Russian poet, translator and writer who published more than two hundred fables.

Kube, Wilhelm (1887–1943) Nazi SS official who was appointed as the General Kommissar for Belarus in July 1941. In September 1943, Kube was assassinated by his maid, Yelena Mazanik, who had worked with Belorussian partisans to coordinate the attack. Mazanik was later honoured with the distinction of Hero of the Soviet Union.

landsleit (Yiddish; in English, landsman) A member of a group who comes from the same town.

landsmanshaftn (Yiddish; in English, hometown societies) Groups of Jewish immigrants from the same towns, cities or regions in eastern and central Europe. In North America, Jewish immigrants often joined these organizations for support and a social network.

Lenin, Vladimir (1870–1924) The founder of the Russian Communist Party and leader of the Bolsheviks throughout the October Revolution in 1917 and Russian Civil War (1917–1923). Lenin is considered the architect of the USSR (Union of Soviet Socialist Republics).

Lohse, Hinrich (1896–1964) Nazi party official who was appointed Reichskommissar (governor) for the Nazi occupation regime in the region named Ostland, which included the Baltic states, northeastern Poland and west Belarus, in July 1941. After the war, Lohse served three years of a ten-year sentence; he was released early due to illness.

Lubavitch A branch of Orthodox, Hasidic Judaism that was founded in Lyubavichi, Lithuania, in the late eighteenth century. The Lubavitch philosophy differs from other Hasidic branches in that it emphasizes intellectual over emotional reasoning. The Lubavitcher Rebbe whom Michael Kutz refers to, also known as Rabbi Menachem Mendel Schneerson (1902–1994), led the Lubavitch movement in New York from 1950 to 1992 and was renowned for his leadership, dedication, passion and outreach.

Lubavitcher Rebbe *See* Lubavitch.

maftir (Hebrew; concluder) Refers to both the last person called up to read the Torah as well as to the Torah portion that is read.

March of the Living An annual event that was established in 1988 and takes place in April on Holocaust Memorial Day (Yom Ha-Shoah) in Poland. The March of the Living program aims to educate primarily Jewish students and young adults from around the world about the Holocaust and Jewish life during World War II. Along with Holocaust survivors, participants march the three kilometres from Auschwitz to Birkenau to commemorate all who perished in the Holocaust. The concept of the event comes from the Nazi death marches that Jews were forced to go on when they were being evacuated from the forced labour and concentration camps at the very end of the war. Many Jews died during these marches and thus the March of the Living was created to both remember and serve as a contrast to this history by celebrating Jewish life and strength. After spending time in Poland, participants travel to Israel and join in celebrations there for Israel's remembrance and independence days.

Masada An ancient fortification in the Judaean Desert in southern Israel that is a UNESCO World Heritage site. Masada was a significant symbol of Jewish rebellion at the end of the First Jewish-Roman War (66–73 CE), when 967 Jews held out against a Roman siege for three years at the top of the fortress. As it became evident that the Romans would prevail, most of the fighters, rather than be taken hostage by the Romans and sold as slaves, agreed to a suicide pact.

matzah (Hebrew; also matza, matzoh, matsah; in Yiddish, matze) Crisp flatbread made of plain white flour and water that is not allowed to rise before or during baking. Matzah is the substitute for bread during the Jewish holiday of Passover, when eating bread and leavened products is forbidden. *See also* Passover.

Megillah The scroll of the Book of Esther, which is traditionally read during the holiday of Purim. *See also* Purim.

Mikhoels, Solomon *See* Jewish Anti-Fascist Committee.

mikvah (Hebrew; literally, a pool or gathering of water) A ritual purification bath taken by Jews on occasions that denote change, such as before the Sabbath (signifying the shift from a regular weekday to a holy day of rest), as well as those that denote a change in personal status, such as before a person's wedding or, for a married woman, after menstruation. The word mikvah refers to both the pool of water and the building that houses the ritual bath.

Minsk ghetto An area in northwestern Minsk established by the Nazis in July 1941, where 80,000 Jews were held. One month later, a resistance group formed in the ghetto and organized escapes to the surrounding forests. Over the course of the ghetto's existence approximately 10,000 Jews were able to escape the ghetto, about half of whom survived and joined the partisans. The ghetto was liquidated in October 1943 and the remaining Jews were deported to either the Sobibor or Maly Trostinets death camps. *See also* partisans.

Mizrachi (acronym of Merkaz Ruchani; Hebrew, spiritual centre) An Orthodox nationalist Zionist movement founded in Vilna, Lithuania in 1902. Mizrachi was founded on the belief that the Torah is central to Zionism and Jewish life. The movement's principles are encompassed in its slogan, "The land of Israel for the people of Israel according to the Torah of Israel." *See also* Zionism.

Molotov-Ribbentrop Pact *See* Treaty of Non-Aggression between Germany and the USSR.

Montgomery, Bernard (1887–1976) British Field Marshal during World War II who was the commander of Allied ground forces during the invasion of Normandy, France on D-Day, June 6, 1944.

NKVD (Russian) The acronym of the Narodnyi Komissariat Vnutrennikh Del, meaning People's Commissariat for Internal Affairs. The NKVD functioned as the Soviet Union's security agency, secret police and intelligence agency from 1934 to 1954. The NKVD's Main Directorate for State Security (GUGB) was the forerunner of the Committee for State Security, better known as the KGB (acronym for Komitet Gosudarstvennoy Bezopasnosti) established in 1954. The organization's stated dual purpose was to defend the USSR from external dangers from foreign powers and to protect the Communist Party from perceived dangers within. Under Stalin, the pursuit of imagined conspiracies against the state became a central focus and the NKVD played a critical role in suppressing political dissent. *See also* Stalin, Joseph.

Orthodox Judaism The set of beliefs and practices of Jews for whom the observance of Jewish law is closely connected to faith; it is characterized by strict religious observance of Jewish dietary laws, restrictions on work on the Sabbath and holidays, and a modest code of dress.

otriad (Russian) A partisan detachment.

partisans Members of irregular military forces or resistance movements formed to oppose armies of occupation. During World War II there were a number of different partisan groups that opposed both the Nazis and their collaborators in several countries. The term partisan could include highly organized, almost paramilitary groups such as the Red Army partisans; ad hoc groups bent more on survival than resistance; and roving groups of bandits who plundered what they could from all sides during the war.

Passover One of the major festivals of the Jewish calendar, Passover takes place over eight days in the spring. One of the main observances of the holiday is to recount the story of Exodus, the Jews' flight from slavery in Egypt, at a ritual meal called a seder. The name itself refers to the fact that God "passed over" the houses of the Jews when he set about slaying the firstborn sons of Egypt as the last of the ten plagues aimed at convincing Pharoah to free the Jews. *See also* matzah; seder.

Poalei Zion (Hebrew, also Poale Zion; Workers of Zion) A Marxist-Jewish Zionist movement founded in the Russian Empire in the early twentieth century.

pogrom (Russian; to wreak havoc, to demolish) A violent attack on a distinct ethnic group. The term most commonly refers to nineteenth- and twentieth- century attacks on Jews in the Russian Empire. *See also* Kristallnacht.

Pope Pius XII (1876–1958) The head of the Catholic Church from 1939 until his death. During World War II, although various sources informed the Pope about the Nazi treatment of Jews in Europe, he never spoke out and condemned the atrocities against Jews specifically. The Pope's official position was one of "neutrality," and in December 1942 he publicly spoke out against horrors that were being committed against people in general. The Pope did protest the 1944 deportations of Jews from Hungary, and over the course of the war, the Vatican hid 477 Jews. His stance during the Holocaust remains controversial.

Purim (Hebrew; literally, lots) The celebration of the Jews' escape from annihilation in Persia. The Purim story recounts how Haman, advisor to the King of Persia, planned to rid Persia of Jews, and how Queen Esther and her cousin Mordecai foiled Haman's plot by convincing the king to save the Jews. During the Purim festivities, people dress up as one of the figures in the Purim story, hold parades and retell the story of Haman, Esther and Mordecai. *See also* grager; Megillah.

refusenik The term applied to people, most often Soviet Jews, who were refused permission to emigrate from the Soviet Union because the regime viewed them as traitors and an imagined threat to state security.

Reichskommissariat Ostland The Nazi civilian occupation administration that ruled Estonia, Latvia, Lithuania, northeastern Poland and western Belorussia during World War II. *See also* Lohse, Hinrich.

Righteous Among the Nations A title bestowed by Yad Vashem, the Holocaust Martyrs' and Heroes' Remembrance Authority in Jerusalem, to honour non-Jews who risked their lives to help save Jews during the Holocaust. A commission was established in 1963 to award the title. If a person fits certain criteria and the story is carefully corroborated, the honouree is awarded with a medal and certificate and commemorated on the Wall of Honour at the Garden of the Righteous in Jerusalem.

Rokossovsky, Konstantin (1896–1968) Soviet marshal and commander of the Red Army forces liberating Poland, and specifically Warsaw, in 1945. In accordance with Stalin's orders, his forces denied support to the independent Polish Home Army uprising against the German occupiers in Warsaw in 1944. The initiators of the uprising hoped to create an independent Poland, while the Soviet Union insisted on it becoming a Soviet-allied satellite state. Rokossovsky and his army did not liberate Warsaw until January 1945.

royfe (Yiddish) An informal, unlicensed doctor.

seder (Hebrew; literally, order) A ritual family meal celebrated at the beginning of the festival of Passover. *See also* Four Questions; matzah; Passover.

Sephardic (Hebrew) The adjective used to describe Sephardim, Jews of Spanish, Portuguese or North African descent. The word derives from the biblical name for a country that is taken to be Spain.

Sforim, Mendele Mocher (1835–1917) Also known as Sholem Yankev Abramovitsh. An author of both Hebrew and Yiddish works, Sforim is considered to be the founder of Yiddish literature.

shalach-manos (Hebrew; abbreviation of mishloach manos, literally, sending of portions) A gift basket sent on the holiday of Purim. The tradition comes from the Book of Esther and is considered a mitzvah (a good deed) by providing people with food to celebrate the holiday. *See also* Purim.

shames (Yiddish) The caretaker of a synagogue.

Sharansky, Anatoly (Natan) (1948–) Israeli politician and author who, as a former Jewish Soviet *refusenik*, was arrested and imprisoned in 1977 after applying to emigrate in 1973. When he was denied an exit visa, Sharansky became an activist in opposition to Soviet regime emigration policies. After his arrest, he was convicted of treason in 1978 and sentenced to thirteen years in a hard labour camp in Siberia. After much political pressure, Sharansky was released in 1986 and immediately immigrated to Israel. *See also* refusenik.

She'erit Hapletah (Hebrew; surviving remnants) A common postwar term for Holocaust survivors. The term, which connotes strength, comes from a biblical concept that can be found in the books of Kings, Isaiah and Ezra. Isaiah 37:31, for example, reads: "The surviving remnant of the house of Judah will again take root downward and bear fruit upward."

shegetz A non-Jewish male. The Hebrew origin of the word is "sheketz," meaning "impurity." Modern usage of the term to refer to gentiles can be either humorous or derogatory, depending on the context.

Shema Yisrael (Hebrew; "Hear, O Israel") The first two words of a section of the Torah and an extremely important prayer in Judaism. The full verse, "Hear, O Israel: the Lord is our God, the Lord is one," refers to faith and loyalty in one God, which is the essence of Judaism. The Shema prayer comprises three verses in the Torah and observant Jews recite the Shema twice daily, in the morning and evening.

Sikorski, Władysław (1881–1943) Prime minister of the Polish government-in-exile in London from 1939 until his death in 1943, and commander of the Polish armed forces in France. In 1941, Sikorski re-established diplomatic relations with the Soviet Union, which led to an amnesty for thousands of Polish and Jewish citizens who were being held prisoner in Soviet forced labour camps. On being released from the camps, many joined the newly formed army that became known as Anders' Army. Sikorski died in a plane crash in July 1943. *See also* Anders' Army.

Simchat Torah (Hebrew; literally, rejoicing in the Torah) The holiday that marks the conclusion of the annual cycle of readings from the Torah and the beginning of a new cycle. The holiday is celebrated in synagogue by singing and dancing with the Torah scrolls.

spekulant (Russian; pl. *spekulanty*) The Soviet term for someone selling something for profit. In the USSR, free market activity was considered anathema to both communist ideology and the centrally planned, state-controlled economy that was the cornerstone of the Soviet system. The intent to resell anything for profit – speculating – was a very serious crime. A *spekulant* was considered to be a "parasite" working in opposition to the "socially useful labour" that was the duty of every Soviet citizen, and was therefore seen as an enemy of the state.

SS (abbreviation of Schutzstaffel; Defence Corps) The SS was established in 1925 as Adolf Hitler's elite corps of personal bodyguards. Under the direction of Heinrich Himmler, its membership grew from 280 in 1929 to 50,000 when the Nazis came to power in 1933, and to nearly a quarter of a million on the eve of World War II. The SS was comprised of the Allgemeine-SS (General SS) and the Waffen-SS (Armed, or Combat SS). The General SS dealt with policing and the enforcement of Nazi racial policies in Germany and the Nazi-occupied countries. An important unit within the SS was the Reichssicherheitshauptamt (RSHA, the Central Office of Reich Security), whose responsibility included the Gestapo (Geheime Staatspolizei). The SS ran the concentration and death camps, with all their associated economic enterprises, and also fielded its own Waffen-SS military divisions, including some recruited from the occupied countries.

Stalin, Joseph (1878–1953) The leader of the Soviet Union from 1924 until his death in 1953. Born Joseph Vissarionovich Dzhugashvili, he changed his name to Stalin (literally: man of steel) in 1903. He was a staunch supporter of Lenin, taking control of the Communist Party upon Lenin's death. Very soon after acquiring leadership of the Communist Party, Stalin ousted rivals, killed opponents in purges, and effectively established himself as a dictator. During the late 1930s, Stalin commenced "The Great Purge," during which he targeted and disposed of elements within the Communist Party that he deemed to be a threat to the stability of the Soviet Union. These purges extended to both military and civilian society, and millions of people were incarcerated or exiled to harsh labour camps. During the war and in the immediate post-war period, many Jews in Poland viewed Stalin as the leader of the country that liberated them and saved them from death at the hands of the Nazis. At the time, many people were unaware of the extent of Stalin's own murderous policies. After World War II, Stalin set up Communist governments controlled by Moscow in many Eastern European states bordering and close to the USSR, and instituted antisemitic campaigns and purges. *See also* Kamenev, Lev; Zinoviev; Grigory.

Star of David (in Hebrew, Magen David) The six-pointed star that is the ancient and most recognizable symbol of Judaism. During World War II, Jews in Nazi-occupied areas were frequently forced to wear a badge or armband with the Star of David on it as an identifying mark of their lesser status and to single them out as targets for persecution.

Stern gang The British name for the radical Jewish paramilitary and Zionist group in British Mandate Palestine led by Avraham Stern called Lehi (in Hebrew, *Lohamei Herut Israel*, meaning Fighters for the Freedom of Israel). Lehi, which advocated for a Jewish state and open immigration for European Jewish refugees, split from the military organization Irgun in 1940 due to disagreement over armed conflict against the British, which Lehi supported and enacted. *See also* British Mandate Palestine; Irgun.

Stewart, Alistair (1905–1970) Member of Parliament for Winnipeg North in the Canadian House of Commons from 1945 to 1958.

tallis (Yiddish; in Hebrew, *tallit*) Jewish prayer shawl traditionally worn during morning prayers and on the Day of Atonement (Yom Kippur). One usually wears the *tallis* over one's shoulders but some choose to place it over their heads to express awe in the presence of God.

Talmud (Hebrew; literally, instruction or learning) An ancient rabbinic text that discusses Jewish history, law and ethics, the Talmud is comprised of two sections: the Mishnah, which is further subdivided into six sections and focuses on legal issues, and the Gemara, which analyzes the legal issues. *See also* Torah.

Tanach (Hebrew, also Tanakh) The Hebrew bible. The word is an acronym of the Hebrew letters that comprise the scriptures; "T" from Torah; "N" from Nevi'im (prophets); and "K" for Ketuvim (writings). *See also* Torah.

tefillin (Hebrew) Phylacteries. A pair of black leather boxes containing scrolls of parchment inscribed with Bible verses and worn by Jews on the arm and forehead at prescribed times of prayer as a symbol of the covenantal relationship with God.

Torah (Hebrew) The Five Books of Moses (the first five books of the Bible), also called the Pentateuch. The Torah is the core of Jewish scripture, traditionally believed to have been given to Moses on Mount Sinai. In Christianity it is referred to as the "Old Testament." *See also* Talmud.

Treaty of Non-Aggression between Germany and the U S S R The treaty that was signed on August 24, 1939, colloquially known as the Molotov-Ribbentrop Pact after signatories Soviet foreign minister Vyacheslav Molotov and German foreign minister Joachim von Ribbentrop. The main provisions of the pact stipulated that the two countries would not go to war with each other and that they would both remain neutral if either one was attacked by a third party. One of the key components of the treaty was the division of various independent countries – including Poland – into Nazi and Soviet spheres of influence and areas of occupation. The Nazis breached the pact by launching a major offensive against the Soviet Union on June 22, 1941.

Tsar Alexander II (1818–1881) Also known as Alexander of Russia, the emperor of Russia from 1855 until his assassination in 1881.

Tsar Nicholas I (1796–1855) Emperor of Russia from 1825 to 1855.

tsitsis (Yiddish pronunciation; in Hebrew, *tzitzit*) The fringes worn by observant Jews, usually attached to a *tallis*. *See also* tallis.

Tu b'Shvat (Hebrew) The holiday that marks the new year for trees. The origin of Tu b'Shvat comes from an ancient custom of calculating the age of a fruit-bearing tree, which was done for the purpose of tithing. Present-day celebrations of the holiday generally focus on planting new trees or eating fruits typically grown in Israel, such as figs and dates.

United Nations Relief and Rehabilitation Administration (U N R R A) An international relief agency created at a 44-nation conference in Washington, DC on November 9, 1943, to provide economic assistance and basic necessities to war refugees. It was especially active in repatriating and assisting refugees in the formerly Nazi-occupied European nations immediately after World War II.

Volksdeutsche (German) The term used by the Nazis to refer to the ethnic Germans living outside Germany in Central and Eastern Europe. Prior to World War II, there were more than 10 million ethnic Germans living in these countries, some of whose families had been there for centuries. When the Nazis occupied these territories, they intended to reclaim the *Volksdeutsche* as Germans and strengthen their communities as a central part of creating the Nazis' ideal of a Greater Germany. Ethnic Germans were often given the choice to either sign the *Volksliste*, the list of German people, and be regarded as traitors by their home countries, or not to sign and be treated as traitors to the "Germanic race" by the Nazi occupiers. After the collapse of Nazi Germany most *Volksdeutsche* were persecuted by the post-war authorities in their home countries.

Wasilewska, Wanda (1905–1964) Polish-born author and political activist who helped establish the Soviet-led First Polish Army between 1943 and 1944. Wasilewska, who became a Soviet citizen in 1939 through the partition of Poland, was an ardent communist and was assigned a seat in Stalin's government in 1940. She became a colonel in the Red Army in 1941, president of the Union of Polish Patriots in 1943 and head of a Soviet provisional government established to control Poland in 1944.

Wehrmacht (German) The German army during the Third Reich.

White Paper A British policy restricting Jewish immigration that was first enacted during the mandate in Palestine in 1939. After the war, the Anglo-American Committee of Inquiry was established to set conditions for Jewish immigration to British Mandate Palestine. One of the conditions in this April 1946 White Paper, which would allow for the immigration of 100,000 Jewish refugees, required the disarming of forces considered illegal by the British authorities. As a result, the policy was rejected by both Arab and Jewish leaders in Palestine.

Yad Vashem The Holocaust Martyrs' and Heroes' Remembrance Authority established in 1953 to commemorate, educate the public about, research and document the Holocaust.

yeshiva (Hebrew) A Jewish educational institution in which religious texts such as the Torah and Talmud are studied. The yeshiva in Mir that Michael Kutz mentions was founded in 1814 and was renowned for its education. During World War II, the yeshiva community first moved to safety in Lithuania and then eventually sought refuge in Shanghai, China. After the war, branches of the Mir yeshiva opened in both Brooklyn and Jerusalem; both still exist today. *See also* Talmud; Torah.

Yiddish A language derived from Middle High German with elements of Hebrew, Aramaic, Romance and Slavic languages, and written in Hebrew characters. Spoken by Jews in east-central Europe for roughly a thousand years from the tenth century to the mid-twentieth century, it was still the most common language among European Jews until the outbreak of World War II. There are similarities between Yiddish and contemporary German.

Yishuv The Jewish community in Israel.

Young Pioneers The Young Pioneer Organization of the Soviet Union, also called the Lenin All-Union Pioneer Organization, was a mass youth organization that instilled communist ideology in Soviet children ages ten to fifteen. Following their participation in the Young Pioneers, adolescents typically joined the Komsomol. *See also* Komsomol.

Zhukov, Georgy (1896–1974) Soviet Red Army commander and marshal of the Soviet Union who led the defense of both Moscow and Stalingrad during World War II, and lifted the siege of Leningrad (St. Petersburg) on January 27, 1944. Zhukov, credited with liberating the Soviet Union and eastern Poland, also led offensives in Belorussia as well as the final battle leading to the surrender of Berlin in April 1945.

Zinoviev, Grigory (1883–1936) Soviet-Jewish Bolshevik politician who was a key member of the Central Committee of the Communist Party on and off from 1917 to 1934. Along with his close colleague Lev Kamenev, Zinoviev was arrested on false charges in 1934 and was victim to one of Stalin's infamous show trials in 1935. He was executed on August 25, 1936. *See also* Kamenev, Lev; Stalin, Joseph.

Zionism A movement promoted by the Viennese Jewish journalist Theodor Herzl, who argued in his 1896 book *Der Judenstaat* (The Jewish State) that the best way to resolve the problem of anti-semitism and persecution of Jews in Europe was to create an independent Jewish state in the historic Jewish homeland of Biblical Israel. Zionists also promoted the revival of Hebrew as a Jewish national language.

Zionist movements in Poland Among the significant Jewish political movements that flourished in Poland before World War II were various Zionist parties – the General Zionists; the Labour Zionists (Poale Zion); the Revisionist Zionists formed under Ze'ev Jabotinsky; and the Orthodox Religious Zionists (the Mizrachi movement) – and the entirely secular and socialist Jewish Workers' Alliance, known as the Bund. Although Zionism and Bundism were both Jewish national movements and served as Jewish political parties in interwar Poland, Zionism advocated a Jewish national homeland in the Land of Israel, while Bundism advocated Jewish cultural autonomy in the Diaspora. A significant number of Polish Jews in the interwar years preferred to affiliate with the non-Zionist religious Orthodox party, Agudath Israel.

Photographs

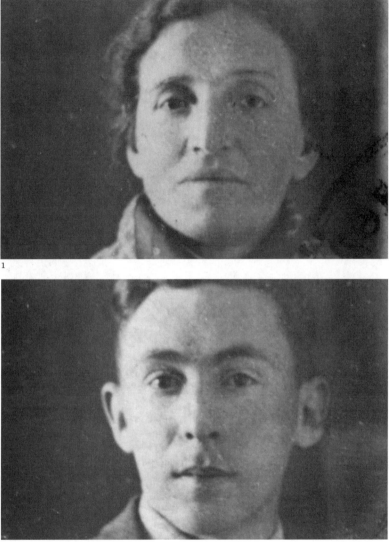

1

2

1 Michael's mother, Ida Zaturensky Kutz, circa 1940.
2 Michael Kutz's older brother, Tsalia, circa 1940.

Michael at age thirteen in his hometown after liberation. Fourth from the left, he and the small group of Nieśwież survivors are standing in front of the town's destroyed main synagogue. Nieśwież, circa 1944. Photo courtesy of Yad Vashem.

1 Michael, front row, second from the left, with a group of Jewish partisans after the war. Lodz, circa 1945.
2 Michael (front row, on the right) with the partisans. Lodz, circa 1945.
3 Fifteen-year-old Michael with a woman from Bricha. Lodz, 1945.
4 With partisan friends in Lodz, 1945.

1 Michael (left) with a friend from the Jewish underground. Italy, circa 1947.
2 Michael in Torino, Italy. 1947.
3 Walking at the far right, Michael at a demonstration against British Mandate policies in Palestine in the Grugliasco DP camp near Torino. 1947.
4 Michael (right) holding a sign during one of the protests.

1 Standing in front of the Kotel, the Western Wall, before his bar mitzvah. February 8, 1990, Jerusalem.

2 Tefillin being wrapped around Michael's arm in preparation for his bar mitzvah. Jerusalem, 1990.

Wearing his medal when he served as Grand chancellor of the Knights of Pythias. Montreal, 1987.

Michael with Rose Parker at a Winnipeg reunion of the group who travelled to Canada with him after the war. Rose was the Jewish Immigrant Aid Society social worker who settled him with the Glassman family in Winnipeg in 1948. Winnipeg, 2002.

Michael in his war veteran uniform for the Brigadier Frederick Kisch branch 97 in Côte St-Luc. Montreal, 2011.

1 Michael and Patricia Kutz's family at their grandson Rhys's bar mitzvah. Left to right: their grandson Joseph; Rhys; their son, Randall Becker; and their daughter-in-law, Kristen Whitehead. Toronto, June 2010.

2 Michael and Patricia Kutz's granddaughter Orion's bat mitzvah. Left to right: their daughter, Judith Becker Charron; their grandson Adam; Orion; and their son-in-law, Andrew Charron. Toronto, April 2011.

Michael and Patricia Kutz, 2011.

Index

The Azrieli Foundation was established in 1989 to realize and extend the philanthropic vision of David J. Azrieli, C.M., C.Q., M.Arch. The Foundation's mission is to support a wide spectrum of initiatives in education and research. The Azrieli Foundation is an active supporter of programs in the fields of Jewish education, the education of architects, scientific and medical research, and education in the arts. The Azrieli Foundation's many well-known initiatives include: the Holocaust Survivor Memoirs Program, which collects, preserves, publishes and distributes the written memoirs of survivors in Canada; the Azrieli Institute for Educational Empowerment, an innovative program successfully working to keep at-risk youth in school; and the Azrieli Fellows Program, which promotes academic excellence and leadership on the graduate level at Israeli universities.